Snickers from the Front Pew

BY

TODD AND JEDD HAFER

Guideposts
New York, New York

This Guideposts edition is published by special arrangement with Todd and Jedd Hafer.

Snickers from the Front Pew
ISBN 1-56292-578-4
Copyright © 2000 by Todd and Jedd Hafer
Published by Honor Books
P. O. Box 55388
Tulsa, Oklahoma 74155

Illustrated by Brant Schelhaas, Littleton, Colorado

Foreword

Church is many things. Sometimes it's somber. Sometimes it's invigorating. Sometimes it's boring. Sometimes it's downright good. But sometimes church is funny. Mainly because churches are filled with imperfect people. And imperfection makes for a lot of funny moments and fond memories.

Those of us who were raised in church can easily relate to these stories by Todd and Jedd Hafer. And people who weren't raised in church will get a kick out of this book, too, because *Snickers from the Front Pew* is about people—people in the lives of the Hafer boys.

Humor is all around us. We just have to open our eyes and look. Some of the things we're crying about today, we'll be laughing about in ten years. So, I say . . . LAUGH NOW! Why wait? Laughter is a great healer. Proverbs calls it a medicine. And everybody could use a good, hard laugh. I believe God loves to hear His children laugh. What healthy father doesn't?

So read on and snicker, laugh, chuckle. And if you feel like it, throw your head back and guffaw!

—Mark Lowry

Acknowledgments

The authors gratefully acknowledge the individuals who made this book possible. First, we acknowledge whoever invented written language. And the folks who invented paper and ink and book glue—they're pretty important, too.

We also thank you, the humor-reading public. Thanks for buying this book. Or for accepting it as a gift and not returning it for a snorkel or pair of tube socks. We hope *Snickers from the Front Pew* makes you laugh so hard that orange juice comes out of your nose—whether you're an orange juice drinker or not. And remember, we need you. We can't spell funny without U!

Most of all, we thank our editor, Rebecca Currington, and the great people at Honor Books for giving us a chance to address Christendom's crying need for laughter. We won't forget your courage in taking a chance on us. We also appreciate Mark Lowry and all the gracious people who said kind things about this book. And we hope the yard work and shower regrouting we did for all of you was satisfactory.

A big thanks goes out to our main, comedic inspirations, especially Ron Hafer, Robin Murray Krug, Keith Stubbs, and Bobo the Juggling Woodchuck.

Finally, we thank our families, especially our wives who said, "You sure enough better acknowledge us, you lightweight funny-boys!"

Introduction

You know what they say about preachers' kids, don't you? Well if you know the answer to that question, you're way ahead of us. You see, we are a preacher's kids, but we don't know what people say about us because parishioners have always whispered in our presence, sometimes laughing or shaking their heads in bewilderment. So as we grew up, we also grew paranoid. What were the members of Dad's congregations saying about us?

There was a time when we thought we'd happened on something. Jedd heard someone whisper, "The apple doesn't fall far from the tree." But our brother Chadd disproved this axiom one day when we were jumping from a twenty-two-foot-high tree branch onto a trampoline. He missed the trampoline and bruised most of his internal organs.

Chadd's mishap made us think. First, we thought that he should have allowed for the strong winds that were blowing and that he shouldn't have attempted a back flip. But we also wondered what other misconceptions people held about preachers' offspring. And we wondered what we could do to address the misconceptions without plunging to the ground from great heights.

Ultimately, we decided that a book was the safest and most logical way to part the velvet curtains and give folks our perspective, our "view from the pew," if you will. (And we're certain you will.)

We've seen some amazing stuff during our P.K. years, and we hope you will enjoy this insiders' view of church life and other related subjects. Before we move on to chapter 1, however, we need to make a few disclaimers and ambiguous remarks:

1. The stories you are about to read are true—pretty much. Sure, there are some embellishments here and there, but we have done this only after much fasting and soul-searching. And even then, we didn't spice up a story unless we could look each other in the eye and face the question: "Will changing this story make it funnier?"

2. The people in these stories are real, except for Todd's imaginary childhood friend, Cowboy Sam. However, we've changed many of the names to protect the identities of certain individuals and save them from utter shame and humiliation. As you will soon discover, some of these people are flakier than a croissant.

3. We've been in a lot of churches. After all, pastors tend to change congregations as often as major-league baseball teams change relief pitchers. But for the sake of simplicity, we've condensed our church-related adventures into one: Broomfield Baptist Church. We did this for two reasons. First, it's the first church we remember anything about. Second, it's much shorter than Broomfield/Enid/Cheyenne/Denver/Colorado Springs/Wellington/Buffalo/Green Mountain Falls/Woodland Park Community Grace Fellowship Presbyterian Baptist Church and Home for Troubled Youth.

Dedication

We dedicate *Snickers from the Front Pew* to our dad, The Reverend Del "Pops" Hafer. Dad is the only 6'2", 270-pound, weight-lifting champion, former semi-pro-football-playing preacher we know. He's also the best preacher we know. As you'll read, he has a unique approach to life, pastoring, fashion, and household repairs, but we respect his commitment to his calling and his courage to do whatever his job required—even if it meant sheltering a wife from an abusive husband or singing an a cappella solo during morning worship when the scheduled musical guest canceled.

This book is also for our Mom, Cherie Hafer, who has endured Old-Testament-style tribulations with grace and humor. And Mom, our love and prayers are with you as you battle cancer. Your opponent is daunting, but victory will be yours.

We would like to include all the other pastors in our family as well. They are: The Reverend Chadd Hafer, Chaplain Ron Hafer, The Reverend Jerry Springston, Chaplain Jay Hafer, and The Almost Reverend-Bradd Hafer, who ministers to needy children through Compassion International, and without whom some of our favorite stories would not have been possible.

In fact we dedicate this book to all pastors and their families. And to the fine people who fill the pews week after week in an incredible display of good faith and commitment. May God bless you for your faithfulness.

Table of Contents

If you ever visit our church, Dad's jacket is the
first thing you'll notice: purple and green
double-knit polyester; big ivory moose-head-
shaped buttons; a Canadian landscape on
the back; pockets large enough to hold
quarter-pounders—hence the grease stains.

Dad's Coat of Many Horrors:
Making the Ministry's Worst-Dressed List

W e're often asked, "What's the most embarrassing thing about being P.K.'s?" Some people think that it's having Dad use a bed-wetting problem in his sermon about "The Great Drought in the Land of Canaan."

Others think it might be when the head deacon stood up in front of the entire congregation and asked, "Todd, was that a holy kiss you were giving my daughter on the front porch last night? Why are you turning red there, boy?"

But truth to tell, what has caused us the most shame is Dad's favorite Sunday preachin' jacket. We're still not sure where he got this piece of apparel. We think it might have been from Winko's Shop for the Tall or Husky Clown.

If you ever visit our church, the jacket is the first thing you'll notice: purple and green double-knit polyester; big ivory moose-head-shaped buttons down the front; a Canadian landscape on the back; and pockets large enough to hold three quarter pounders—hence, the grease stains.

Over the years, we've hidden the jacket we nicknamed "The Coat of Many Horrors." But Dad always finds it. (One of the woodchucks in the Canadian landscape scene has glow-in-the-dark eyes.)

We tried milder forms of dissuasion, too: "Wow Dad that coat is really kinda out of style."

"What? I'll have you know Mrs. Fargutson complimented me on this coat just last Sunday," he would counter. "Good thing someone has some fashion sense around here."

"But Dad," we would wail, "Mrs. Fargutson is eighty years old and wears white go-go boots and a straw hat with plastic fruit on it."

"What's wrong with that? Kind of reminds people of the fruit of the Spirit. Now that you mention it, I may use her hat as a visual aid next Sunday. Hey, thanks guys. That was very helpful."

We're still not sure where he got this piece of apparel. We think it might have been from Winko's Shop for the Tall or Husky Clown.

Finally realizing that logic had sorely failed us, we were forced to resort to sabotage. Extreme measures were in order. Frankly, it took Todd a few minutes to come to grips with a more drastic solution. He's always been a bit squeamish about doing things that can conceivably alter the course of history. But finally even Todd had to bow to the gravity of the situation. So one Wednesday night while Dad was over at the church for Bible study, we took the "Coat of Many Horrors" and dropped it off at Goodwill.

Imagine our consternation when we found it lying on the porch the next morning with a death-threat letter pinned to the lapel. We don't want to cast aspersions on a fine charitable organization, but that, friends, is *not* good will! (Calm down, folks. We made that last part up.)

This incident has brought us to a place of acceptance, however. Obviously, the "Coat of Many Horrors" has its own special place in the wide spectrum of God's mysterious ways. We're trying to be philosophical about it—at least Dad hasn't tried to squeeze into his 1970s white-and-purple-striped bell-bottoms . . . yet.

The Agape basketball team featured athletic
Bible college students and no fat old guys.
This directly violated the unwritten code of
church-league basketball: Every team must have
a minimum of two fat old guys, with corrective
lenses and at least one knee brace per geezer.

Church Basketball:
Throwing Up a Prayer

A long time ago, someone decided that a little sweaty competition among church congregations would be healthy, fun, and spiritually enriching. Shortly after that idea was dismissed, someone else came up with the concept of "church league basketball."

A church basketball league is just like a regular league, except that the players are in poorer shape and have to come up with creative expletives like "sugar! golly-darn!" or "great gallopin' googly-moogly" when they miss a shot or fire a chest-pass into a teammate's groin. Some churches have gyms in which they can practice. Others, like Broomfield Baptist Church, practice in a driveway with a twelve-degree slant and a crooked nine-foot basket with no net.

But BBC does have the Hafer Boys—four strapping young men (we were always getting strapped for something) eager for some holy hoop-la. Since we are all well over six feet—except for one brother who for the sake of example we'll call Chadd—we are expected to play starring roles and lead the team to the league championship.

Unfortunately while we have talent for folding bulletins and lip-synching hymns, we don't exactly play like Doctor J. In fact, we play more like Doctor Quinn, Medicine Woman. We take comfort, however, because no one else in the church league can play either—except for those Assembly of God cheaters who always bring in several ringers.

After one of these seven-foot behemoths does a 360 slam-dunk on us, we all mutter, "Sure, that guy goes to their church! Nobody who can jump that high even goes to church! He's close enough to God already!"

But we don't want to give the impression that we've been sore losers. Sure, we've been sore. And we do lose—plenty. But we've always enjoyed the competition, especially the one year we made it to the finals.

We don't exactly play like Doctor J. In fact, we play more like Doctor Quinn, Medicine Woman.

That was the year Jedd shot up five inches over the summer. (Chadd shrank about one and a half inches over the same span, but cumulatively speaking we gained some key net height.)

The season began beautifully. We creamed the Catholics, pounded the Presbyterians, mauled the Methodists, and edged the Episcopalians. But our winning streak was snapped at the hands of the Agape Ranch (AKA the cheaters we mentioned earlier). We simply had no chance. Their team was composed of athletic Bible college students and no old fat guys. This was in direct violation of the unwritten code of church league basketball: Every team must have a minimum of two old fat guys, preferably with corrective lenses and at least one knee brace per geezer.

Anyway, we rebounded from our defeat and breezed through the rest of the season right into the post-season tournament finals. There, of course, we met Agape again.

Fortunately for us, one of our aged, hefty guys with thick glasses—for the sake of anonymity, we'll call him "Dad"—had a wedding to perform and couldn't make the big game. So, with our chances enhanced, we set about the business of lovingly beating the soup out of these upstart Bible students with their neat little haircuts and forty-inch vertical jumps.

It was a close game. Back and forth. Neck and neck. A barn-burner right down to the wire—and many other sports clichés too numerous to mention. The score was tied 44 to 44 with eight seconds to play, and we had the ball. The crowd, all seventeen people, were on the edge of their seats. Todd lofted a perfect pass to Dave, a deacon with eleven kids and a mean outside jump shot. As the clock ticked down to one second, Dave lofted a desperation shot from the top of the key.

The shot was on line. It arched poetically into the stale air of the Broomfield Community Gymnasium and Bingo Hall. All eyes followed the leather sphere as it went straight into the buck!

No, that's not a typo! The ball stuck fast in the antlers of a giant trophy deer head which peered down from the wall above the backboard. The deer stared menacingly at us as if to say, "You may have shot me, made my body into jerky, and mounted my head up here, but I have your lousy basketball! You stinkin' Bambi killers!"

Of course the game stopped right there "dead on the wall" so to speak since that was our only basketball. As we pondered our situation, Dad walked into the gym with grains of wedding rice sprinkled in his hair. He looked at the scoreboard, then at the buck.

"It appears," he said, "that we're on the horns of a dilemma."

Dave spoke up, "I don't mean to be disrespectful, Pastor, but I think that's actually a deer, not a dilemma. Them dilemmas, they got short, curly horns and live in Australia or the Ozarks or somethin'."

We all looked at Dave in wide-eyed bewilderment— even the deer. Then the conversation returned to which team should be crowned league champions. The Agape-ites claimed they should get the first-place trophy because they beat us in the regular season. We, of course, pooh-poohed that approach, arguing that when playoff time comes you can throw the regular season right out the window. Dave quickly pointed out that the gym didn't have any windows.

Dad stroked his chin for a moment before plucking a grain of rice from his hair and nibbling on it thoughtfully. Then with Solomon-like wisdom, he spoke, "Well, this dilemma—I mean situation—reminds me of something from the Old Testament."

He strolled to the scorer's table and lifted the handsome chrome-plated trophy which featured an eight-inch hoopster frozen in mid jump shot. It was quite striking. "Tell you what I'm gonna do," Dad began. "Since both of you want this precious trophy so much, let's just cut it in half. That way each team can share the glory. Sure, the trophy will be grotesquely disfigured and forever a monument to both teams' selfishness, but that's just fine with me. If neither side can give a little here, I see no other recourse."

Of course we Hafer boys could see right away that Dad was going for the Solomon-and-the-baby principle. He fully expected his boys to do the right thing and set an example of humility and grace that would be remembered as long as out-of-shape Christians gather in musty gymnasiums to battle on the hardwood.

Dad smiled at us knowingly. "So, guys, what should I do? Give this trophy to Agape or go get the hacksaw?"

* * * * * * * *

The trophy case at Broomfield Baptist Church is small. There's a bowling plaque, some perfect-attendance certificates, and one third-place ribbon from the 1973 all-church tug-o'-war. There isn't really enough room for a whole basketball trophy in there anyway.

But half a trophy fits just fine. And thanks to the fact that we shrewdly chose "heads" rather than "tails" in the ensuing coin toss, we got the half of the guy that's holding the basketball! Sure, we know what you're thinking: *Isn't half a trophy somewhat unwieldy?* Okay, it toppled over on the bowling trophy a few times, but we quickly discovered how to prop up our half-hoopster with a twenty-two-ounce can of creamed corn.

Next season, we plan to win a whole trophy. You see, some of those guys from Air Agape are graduating from Bible college and being called away to the mission field. Far away. Whereas the nucleus of our team works at a local feed store. They aren't going anywhere—especially Dave, who's still trying to get his G.E.D. and pass his driver's license test.

So the undisputed championship should one day be ours . . . if we can find a stick long enough to free the basketball from the buck's antlers.

Mayhem in the Manor

Our mom and dad have now been married for more than forty years. This is an astounding feat in today's world, especially when you consider that they have raised four boys; served in more than a dozen churches; owned legions of cats, dogs, reptiles, and amphibians; and moved seventeen times.

We're often asked, "What is your parents' secret? How have they stayed together so long?"

From what we can tell, the secret is to argue . . . a lot. But—and here is the key—argue about life's most insignificant details. Find the most irrelevant matter and battle over it as if it were the last scrap of beef jerky on a desert island. Then you'll lack the desire and the energy to fight about the important stuff. This may seem like a strange tactic, but it works. It's kind of like a flu shot where they inject a little bit of the virus to protect you from the big kung-fu flu. Think of it as preventive bickering.

Perhaps, though, you've been to too many marriage enrichment seminars and have forgotten how to quarrel over life's minutiae. Never fear. Using actual examples from Mom and Pops Hafer's forty-plus years of life together, we now present this refresher course in "Preventive Bickering." Consider, if you will, the following sterling examples!

The Horrific Horn Honk Harangue

Polls are never 100 percent accurate. But we did take a vote, and all four Hafer boys gave the nod to this as Mom and Dad's second dumbest fight ever!

We had just begun a family trip in our luxury '68 Dodge Dart when Dad inadvertently bumped the horn with his elbow. It was just a tiny honk, but that's all a seasoned couple needs.

Mom: Who are you honking at?

Dad: No one.

Mom: You just honked at someone.

Dad: No, I didn't.

Mom: *(Annoyed silence, followed by)* Kids, did you just hear your Dad honk?

Todd: Mom, Dad's not a goose! How could he honk?

Rest of Family: Shut up, Todd.

Mom: Did you kids hear Dad honk the horn or not?

Kids: *(With a deep, collective sigh)* Yeah.

Dad: So?

Mom: So? You just said you didn't honk the horn!

Dad: No, I said I didn't honk at anybody.

Mom: *(Through clenched teeth.)* No, you didn't! You said you didn't honk the horn!

Dad: I never said anything about merely honking the horn. You asked who I honked at, and I said, "No one."

Mom: Kids, did you hear him say . . .

Jedd: *(Then age five)* If you two don't straighten up, we'll turn this car around and go right back home!

Are you beginning to see the genius in their method? But the Horrific Honk Harangue is nothing compared to . . .

It was just a tiny honk, but that's all a seasoned couple needs.

The Bombastic Banana Race

One quiet summer morning, the Hafer family was enjoying breakfast. Mom was being the prototypical Proverbs 31 woman, serving Dad by preparing him a slice of banana bread—the real banana bread. You take a piece of bread. Then you slice bananas and put them on top.

Mom was using her standard technique, hacking the banana into slices and carefully placing each slice on the bread. Unfortunately Dad was ravenous on this particular morning, and that would prove to be his undoing. His hunger drove him to question Mom's technique, and the ensuing encounter went something like this:

Dad: Not to make a big deal of it or anything, but . . . what you're doing there isn't very efficient. If you cut up the whole banana, then put on each slice, you're handling every banana piece twice. A better way would be to slice off one banana piece, so it sticks to the knife, then wipe the slice onto the bread.

Mom: You're wrong. My way's much better.

Dad: *(Forcing a laugh.)* Nope, it isn't. Sorry, but my way's quicker; I'm telling you. You're just not being teachable.

Mom: You think you can teach me about making banana bread? Ha!

At this point, our parents did what any two mature adults would do. They decided to stage a race to see whose banana technique was superior. Eagerly, they each grabbed a banana and a naked piece of bread. Jedd had to say "go" because he was youngest and the threat of "Do this or we're going to turn the puppy over to the pound" scared him the most.

One three-count and they were on their way.

Mom: *(Hack-hack-hack-hack. Place banana. Place banana. Place banana. Place banana.)*

Dad: *(Slice/swipe. Slice/swipe. Slice/swipe.)*

Mom, always insightful, quickly noticed that Dad was edging her. He had only one more row of bananas to slice and swipe. So summoning her last reserve of energy, she chopped the remaining stub of her banana like a crazed beni-hana chef and flung the pieces onto her bread. She struck a blow for women's rights that day. She proved she was a world-class banathlete. And she handled her victory with quiet dignity..

Mom: I WIN! I WIN! I WIN! HA-HA-HA-HA-
HA! Kids, did you see that? I whipped your daddy's
behind really good, didn't I?

*Dad watched Mom's celebration with a smug grin,
shaking his head.*

Dad: Cherie, you didn't win. I'm filing a protest
with the kids.

Mom: What?! A protest? What are you talking
about? You didn't even finish yours!

Dad: Yes, let's talk about my banana bread. It may
be incomplete, but it's neat and orderly. Look at your
bread. Look at the way the bananas are carelessly
piled up in a big heap. Looks like some kind of crude,
pagan, banana altar. I don't think the Lord would be
pleased with that.

Mom: Oh, you're just a sore loser. I win! Don't I,
kids?

Again, the pressure was on us. We conferred briefly.

Chadd: Well, they both spank us.

Bradd: True, Chadd, but Mom is the one who
feeds us. Dad hasn't even figured out how to work the
microwave yet. Every time he tries to heat his coffee,
he resets the clock to Eastern standard time.

We all nodded solemnly at Bradd's wisdom.

Chadd: *(With fervor.)* Mom, you win!

Mom: Whooooo-eeeeeee!

*Standing to her feet, she spiked her banana peel
like a football and did her version of the end-zone dance.*

Dad pounded his fist on the table.

Dad: No fair! I was robbed! This is an outrage!

At that point, the manager of the Village Inn where we were dining came to our table.

Manager: I'm sorry, folks. But I'm going to have to ask you to leave. And, oh yeah, never come back. Please.

We trudged out of the restaurant, dejected. All except for Mom, who, still slightly giddy with victory, insisted on high-fiving a bus-boy on the way out.

How did our parents overcome this bitterly contested banana fiasco? How did their marriage survive such a controversy? Well, when we got home, both were so exhausted that they collapsed together on the couch and fell asleep, Mom nestled on Dad's chest. Not a word was said about how the offerings had been low lately, how we lacked the money to pay that month's bills, or whether Mom should look for a job.

A few hours later, Mom and Dad woke up, smiling sheepishly at each other. "You hungry?" Mom asked Dad.

"I'm famished, honey," he replied. "You know, I could really go for some of your banana bread. . . ."

Leftovers:
The Right Thing to Do

We came in one afternoon and found our mom sitting at the kitchen table, glassy-eyed, no pulse, the works. When we spoke to her, she turned to us with a vacant stare and said, "Boys, I'm just one nerve short of a nervous breakdown."

"Wow!" Todd whispered. "This looks bad. Do you think she found out Chadd shellacked the hamster?"

"Nah," Jedd said. "She's pretty cool about that kind of stuff. I bet this was a job-related trauma."

Just then Mom turned to us and began to speak softly, at first. This is what she said:

"It's always the same. Ding-dong! Ding Dong! You hear the doorbell. You race to the door and peek through the peephole, hoping to see Ed McMahon and the Big Prize Gang. Instead you gaze upon the eager, gaunt faces of one of the church families. Perhaps they've just finished shopping or taking karate lessons. But no matter where they're coming from, they will be hungry. They're always hungry. They'll drop little hints, 'Boy, are we famished! We've been on the go and haven't eaten all day!' Or, 'Nice parakeet. Are they mostly white or dark meat?'

You panic. You can't feed this battalion. You have only one frozen pizza in the freezer. Between these invaders and your own family, everyone would get a piece of pizza the size of a postage stamp. Of course, you could order out for pizza, but you'd have to write the delivery man a check. And your account is already more overdrawn than a 'Where's Waldo?' cartoon.

What is a pastor's wife to do?

Then you remember something. There's a plastic bag in the back of your freezer encased in ice crystals like that woolly mammoth they found back in the 1950s. And wait, there's also a cylindrical foil-wrapped item in your refrigerator's vegetable crisper. And what about the cute little Chinese take-out box? Is it still tucked back there behind the two-gallon jug of chocolate milk?

As your mind races, you realize that you might be able to put together a left-over surprise casserole and satisfy the hunger of your uninvited guests. Your panic begins to subside. You can do this, you tell yourself. There is only one problem: How do you know if your leftovers are church-guest safe? You don't want these people on their knees retching on your carpet or passing nasty rumors around the church about how the pastor and his wife are trying to poison church members."

With that Mom fell silent once more, her energy spent.

"Mom," Todd began, "I think we can help." Then he nudged Bradd and told him to hurry over to the fridge and grab Mom a glass of root beer—straight up, no ice.

As Mom sipped her root beer, the color began to return to her cheeks, and we started to think we might have been responsible for bringing her back from the abyss, as it were. Todd (our very own chronic over-achiever) grabbed some paper and a pen off Dad's desk and said, "Now Mom, we're here for ya, and we're not leaving until we write out some guidelines for food freshness that will leave you feeling much more secure," he announced.

He nudged Bradd and told him to hurry over to the fridge and grab Mom a glass of root beer—straight up, no ice.

We shudder to think what might have happened if we hadn't come in just when we did.

Fortunately a tragedy was averted that day, and now it's time to share our wisdom with the world. After all, we feel it could be helpful in a number of ways, and particularly so for pastors' wives who serve uninvited guests six to eight times a week!

Guidelines For Leftovers

1. Carefully unwrap or uncover the item in question and sniff. If at all possible, the sniffing should be done by a woman. We don't mean to be gender-biased; but, women have superior olfactory skills, just as they have

the inner tracking devices that allow them to answer all variations of the question, "Honey, do you know where my _____ is?" So only women sniff the food carefully. Does the smell match the food item being smelled? For example, if you're sniffing smelt, does the smelt being smelled smell like smelt? Or is it malodorous and foul? Like dead crayfish or dime-store cologne?

Upon smelling, if the food makes you cry like the movie *Terms of Endearment* or the last ten minutes of the "Jerry Lewis Telethon," don't feed it to your guests. It's also a bad sign if your parakeet dies upon exposure. If the food's stench is this bad, it's best to treat it like nuclear waste and don't even put it on your compost heap. After all, maggots have feelings too.

2. Study the food for mold. But please understand that mold has its progressive stages. If the mold is a peaceful seafoam green, flaky, and confined to a small area (like the political clout of the Prohibition Party), it's just stage-one mold. Scrape it off and serve the food— but only to guests with undiscriminating taste buds. If your diners are astronauts, feral children, or insurance salespeople, they probably won't suspect a thing.

Stage-two mold is multi-colored, like one of Elton John's suits. It's also likely to have more hair than Gene Shalit. Trying to extract this mold from food is a messy, tedious job, and what really is the point? If you're truly ambitious, you could try to remove a bit of the mold and rub it on the head of a balding guest. As for the food, don't feed it to anyone or anything, except maybe a vulture, jackal, or linemen from a Big Ten college football team.

Stage-three mold is likely to move and moan angrily, like the blob in that old movie. If this happens, run from your home; move somewhere far away; and leave no forwarding address. It's the only way to escape from stage-three mold, although the drop-in guests will probably track you down—and they'll still be hungry.

3. Packaged foods. The serveability of packaged foods is usually easy to determine. Just check the expiration dates. If Harry S. Truman was still in office, beware. After all, look where Harry S. Truman is today. Generally anything more than a week past its expiration date should be discarded. Possible exceptions include Twinkies, Slim Jims, and Ding-Dongs, which have shelf lives of 2.7 billion years. These items can be served with pride to any and all guests.

4. Chocolate. We're not going to kid you, throwing out chocolate can be painful. However if you have a Hershey bar and can't break it into pieces even with a ball-peen hammer, think twice. There is one exception to this rule: If your guests happen to be women suffering from PMS, get the jack-hammer and do what it takes.

5. A couple of final tips:

Your leftovers will last longer if stored in those handy containers designed for keeping food fresh. Anything that burps is okay.

Pets can be good barometers of food spoilage. If a food item falls to the floor and your dog sniffs it but declines to eat it, you're dealing with something highly toxic. Remember, we are talking about an animal who will gladly drink from the toilet. If you have a pet goat and even he won't eat the item, see our guideline on "stage-three mold."

The Death Limo

We think it was the Catholics who first used buses to carry members to and from church—hence the term "mass transportation." Now every congregation feels it is pretty much essential to obtain a big vehicle to haul its stuff and its people around.

Being a small church, Broomfield Baptist didn't need a whole bus. There were only eight kids in our youth group, and most of the older parishioners owned Novas or Pacers or lived within walking distance.

So for a while, our vehicle of choice was a long, crude-oil black hearse (or "death limo," if you prefer). As kids we loved the hearse, which we affectionately nicknamed "Patty Hearse." All eight youth-groupers fought over which four would get to ride in the very back. The winners would all lie side-by-side like shabbily dressed Mrs. Paul's fish sticks and pretend to be dead. Boy, those were the days.

Patty Hearse was a great mode of transportation. No one ever cut us off at an intersection. No one ever tail-gated us. Perhaps they feared ramming into us and having a corpse pop up in the back. Or maybe it's just that a hearse is a good rolling reminder of where aggressive drivers can end up. We think the government should hire some people to drive corpse coupes around the country. It might work even better than those TV spots featuring country singers: "This is Billy-Bob Dave. I know that most of my songs are about gettin' drunk and drivin' my pickup right through the Dairy Delight. But don't y'all be a-doin' that! Ya hear?"

> The winners would all lie side-by-side like shabbily dressed Mrs. Paul's fish sticks and pretend to be dead.

Anyway, all of us in the youth group looked forward to many years of lying rigid in the back and competing for the coveted "Supreme Stiff Award." These contests were often hotly debated:

Todd: Chadd, I see your chest moving!

Chadd: No, you can't. It's perfectly still. Besides, I saw your left eye twitch!

Todd: Did not!

Chadd: Did, too. You're the worst excuse for a dead guy that I've ever seen!

Todd: You take that back!

Bradd: How could either one of you see anything unless your eyes were open? Huh? Huh!?

Todd and Chadd: We're not talking to you; we're dead!

Our church van, which we named Van Morrison, was never serviced. The engine sounded a lot like a trash compactor. Only Dad and a 300-pound elder named Chet were strong enough to budge Van's transmission.

Church Van:
Unsafe at Any Speed

*U*nfortunately, all our fun crumbled like a too-fresh bran muffin when a new family with two kids joined BBC. With great sadness, we realized that Patty Hearse simply couldn't hold ten little stiffs. We all cried the day Dad had to trade her in.

It took us a while to warm up to the idea of a church van, especially this one. Its exterior was two-tone—seafoam green and off-seafoam green. The front-seat, captain's chairs, had been re-covered in traffic-cone orange vinyl. The second and third row seats were their original avocado color. (Or maybe it was off-off-seafoam green.) The floorboards may or may not have been carpeted. We're not sure because from almost the very beginning, they were littered with cola cans, donut boxes, and a coffee-stained road map of Nebraska.

On the positive side, the van did have a great sound system—an eight-track tape player. And we had a selection of three, count 'em, three tapes from which to choose. There was *Foghat Live,* which came with the van. There was an Evie tape, purchased for us by the Proverbs 31 Tuesday Night Bible Study and Macrame Guild. We're not sure of the title, but it's the one that had the song "I'm only four foot eleven, but I'm going to heaven and that makes me feel ten feet tall." They don't write 'em like that anymore. And, for the rare over-sixty-five passengers, there was *George Beverly Shea's Greatest Hits,* which we won from the Lutherans in a wallyball match.

As far as we know, the van, which we eventually named Van Morrison, was never serviced. The engine sounded a lot like a trash compactor. Also, only Dad and a 300-pound elder named Chet were strong enough to budge Van's manual transmission; and, even with their strength, it took much grinding and gnashing of gears.

There was another reason that Dad was about the only person who could or would drive Van—the inside rear-view mirror was broken off. Dad was trying to adjust it one time, and . . . well, he is a power lifter. He tried to stick the mirror back on the windshield, but there are a few things that even Elmer's glue and lots of hollering won't fix. He did the next best thing, though. He propped the mirror up on the dashboard, wedging it carefully between a hymnal and a crumpled 7-Up can. After the mirror plopped into his lap a few times, he used some of Mom's flannelgraph Old Testament characters to ensure a more snug fit.

Given Van's many problems, we'd often suggest, "Hey, Dad, don't you think we should have this thing checked out? Maybe fixed up a bit?"

"Nah," he'd reply thoughtfully. "You see, kids, a van is a lot like eschatology. It's big and mysterious and you really shouldn't poke around in it too much. You just hope things will work out for the best." At this point in our conversations, we'd all grow quiet and nod our heads. (We had no idea what eschatology was.)

Van had some other minor problems. The speedometer needle was busted. Dad tried to fix it by taping a toothpick to the little orange stub of the needle, but the heavy vibrations from Van's engine always shook the toothpick loose and into the garbage on the floorboard. So we devised a method of guessing our speed. We'd stick our hands out the window and wait for a bug to hit.

If the bug-to-hand impact was mild, like catching an infield pop fly during a church softball game, we'd deduce that Van was doing twenty to thirty miles per hour. If a bug made a loud snap when it hit and stung like a high-five from Muhammad Ali, we'd guess fifty miles per hour. If the bug felt like a white-hot bullet and made us scream like a twelve-year-old girl at an Osmond Brothers concert, we'd put the speed at seventy-one miles per hour and beg Dad to slow down. (By the way, if your speedometer breaks, try this method. Of course, your estimated speed may vary, depending on what kind of bugs are crowding your area roadways.)

You see, kids, a van is a lot like eschatology. It's big and mysterious and you really shouldn't poke around in it too much.

Van's gas gauge was one of the few things that did work properly. But that didn't matter much. The little needle was rarely above the "E" line. You see, after buying his daily dirigible-sized eclairs, Dad usually had only about fifty-eight cents for gas. So we often used the "coast and pray method" of getting around. This method is surprisingly effective. We often rambled for twenty or thirty miles after Van's gas tank was as dry as Margaret Thatcher's sense of humor.

Our most memorable trip in Van occurred in 1983 when Dad drove the whole youth group up into the Colorado mountains for a week-long camp called "God's Li'l Survivalists." The idea was to get closer to God by living in tents and eating tree bark and stuff. Obviously this wasn't the kids' idea. In fact, when the needle dipped below empty twenty miles from the camp and Dad said, "Okay, start praying, kids," none of us did. We just bowed our heads and wondered what tree bark tasted like.

About five miles from our destination, Van planted himself firmly in the middle of the dirt road and refused to coast another foot. "No problem," Dad said cheerfully. "I'll just get out and push. Todd, you and Jedd steer. It'll be a good workout."

Dad had little trouble pushing the hulking "Mean, Seafoam Green Machine." Unfortunately, we weren't as successful with the steering wheel. After we killed two innocent aspen trees, Dad had to switch plans. He got in the van to steer, and we pushed. We made it about a mile—maybe. It's hard to judge distance when every muscle in your body is screaming in pain, and you see white spots jitter-bugging before your eyes.

At that point, we abandoned Van and hiked the rest of the way to camp. Relief washed over us when we saw the crude log-cabin lodge that served as camp headquarters. The relief vanished when we saw the sign in the front window:

Welcome to Camp!
This week's theme: Incontinence & You.

Next Week: God's Li'l Survivalists.

Dad has practically memorized the whole New Testament in Greek. But with dates, he sometimes has a few troubles. So he may have gotten things confused, but we decided to blame the confusion on the church secretary since she took the fall for most of the problems anyway.

After that fiasco, the elders decided to sell Van and try car-pooling. And, hey, if you're the one who bought Van, please give us a call. Mom needs her flannel-graph characters back—the ones Dad used to prop up the rear-view mirror. Mom has an awful time telling the "Fiery Furnace" story in Sunday school without Shadrack and Abednego. "Mrs. Hafer," some kid will always scream, "Did the other two dudes get toasted in the furnace?"

"No," she replies, trying hard to hide the irritation in her voice. "They're on mirror duty in a really ugly van."

The Theological Know-How Dudes, Part *Un!*

*O*kay, we've had some fun up to this point, but some of you may be saying, "I love the laughter and cheer this book has brought me. You could have charged double, and I still would have deemed it the best purchase of my lifetime. I think your royalties should be doubled on your next book. But I want more. After all, life can't be all laughs—unless you're a game-show host. I need some solid Bible teaching."

Never fear. Well, actually, you should fear if you're being chased by rabid hyenas or something, but just don't fear about the Bible teaching part. We know that a book with nothing but humor would be like a cake with nothing but frosting. And a cake like that can give you a whopping stomach ache. We know from experience. So right now we're putting on our Bible-scholar hats (Jedd, your hat's on crooked . . . okay, that's better) and preparing ourselves to answer your deepest, most troubling theological conundrums. Fire away!

Question: We're having our first child—a boy— next month. We'd like to give him a biblical name. We're thinking Matthew. Do you approve?

Answer: No, we're sorry. Matthew is a fine biblical name, but it's too common. These days, every Tom, Dick, and Harry is named Matthew.

Question: We've heard that you are strong advocates of prayer. Do you believe there is anything that prayer can't change?

Answer: You're right about our feelings on prayer. After all, we both took many exams in college, and we're Chicago Cubs fans! We do believe that prayer can change anything—except dirty diapers. That you have to handle yourself.

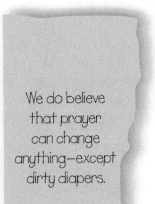

We do believe that prayer can change anything—except dirty diapers.

Question: On the subject of Washington, do you support term limits for Congress?

Answer: No, we do not. We think congresspersons should have to serve their full jail terms, just like other criminals.

Question: Our children really want to trick-or-treat this Halloween, but our church frowns on this holiday. What should we do?

Answer: Boy, that's a tough question. Hmmm. Perhaps a compromise between kids and church would be in order. You could do what our parents always did. We didn't actually get to trick-or-treat. Instead, every year they dressed us up as raccoons and told us to rummage through the neighborhood garbage for our "treats."

Question: I've been to several Christian stores, but I can't find any decent manna. What gives?

Answer: Don't be dismayed. A good manna is hard to find.

Question: I always get confused—when is Easter this year?

Answer: On Easter Sunday.

Question: Okay, but when is National Redundancy Day?

Answer: It will be celebrated on Tuesday, August 22nd, and again on Wednesday, August 23rd. For more information on this holiday, contact The Department of Redundancy Department, New York, New York 10101-0101.

Question: Like you guys, I grew up in a Baptist church, but I've attended several other denominations since then. How do I know if I'm still a real Baptist?

Answer: Just take our "Baptist Self-Test Below." Simply check each item you agree with.

1. The closest I get to dancing is wriggling into my girdle before Easter Service (women only, please).

2. I think Andy Williams would still be a big star if only he'd slowed the tempo a little.

3. I irrigate my lawn rather than using a sprinkler system.

4. I believe pew cushions are for wimps.

5. For me, "wine" in the Bible is properly translated "Welch's 100% Grape Juice."

6. I think that Beethoven was okay, but Fanny Crosby was a real musical genius!

7. I believe that any sermon over before noon ain't a real sermon!

8. Every year at the church carnival, I volunteer to be in the dunk tank.

9. My life's creed: "If the King James Version was good enough for Jesus, it's good enough for me."

10. I think the "luck" in "pot luck" is good!

11. I throw out my swimming suit when it gets a hole in the knee.

12. My idea of a rock group is Mount Rushmore.

If you checked at least ten items, you are a Baptist in good standing. If you checked all twelve, Jerry Falwell would probably like to have you over for dinner. But please call first!

Praying Out Loud for Crying Out Loud

S ooner or later, it will happen to you. It might be at Bible study, or at a church softball game, a potluck dinner. But at some point in your life, you will be singled out to "ask the blessing," "lead us in prayer," or "send one up to The Big Dude Upstairs." And few things are as daunting as being asked to pray out loud.

Praying in private, where only God hears you, is one thing. Praying in the presence of an audience is another. Your spirituality is on the line. Your prayer will be evaluated for its volume, content, dramatic presentation, and length. You don't want people whispering later, "What a tentative, wimpy prayer. Five 'ums, three split infinitives, and no Thous! That poor sap couldn't pray his way out of a wet paper bag!"

We don't want this to happen to you, so here are a few tips to help your next public prayer be loud and proud:

1. **Speak the King's English.** Our years in a Baptist church have taught us that God apparently favors King James lingo. For example, Chet the elder talks this way in casual conversation: "Hey, fellers, how about we go a-wadin' thru the crick for a spell then

head on over to the homestead and fry us up a big honkin' mess o' catfish?"

But when asked to pray, Chet intones something like, "Thou, our Father, we doth beseech and bequest and bequeath to Thee our supplications which we hast gathered as we doth now draweth nigh unto Thine holy presence. And we praiseth Thee, for Thou hast sleweth the uncircumcised Philistines which hath dwelleth southwest of Zion."

When praying aloud, you can gain extra peer points by "lifting someone up," rather than merely praying for him.

We rarely know what Chet is asking (sorry— beseeching), but it sure sounds impressive.

2. **Use a deeper voice.** Again, based on our experience, God will hear you better if you drop your voice an octave or two. If you're a woman, try to sound like Bea Arthur. If you're a husky and daring man, go for James Earl Jones. If you think going that deep will give you the bends, a Johnny-Cash-like rumble will do.

3. **Make liberal use of the words "just" and "really."** If booming KJV-speak just isn't your cup of soup, you can still make your prayer sound earnest and sincere by adding "just" and "really." You see it's not enough to simply ask God to remove Mabel Smigdell's gout. It's better to say with a slight whine in

your voice, "God, we just really pray for Mabel and her gout right now, God. It's really just a bad situation, God. So if You could just really rid her of that really bad gout, we'd just really be thankful to You. Really."

4. **Remember to "lift people up."** When praying aloud, you can gain extra peer points by "lifting someone up," rather than merely praying for him. For example, "We lift up at this time Mr. Meany's cat, Fat Daddy, who has a benign tumor under his tail. And we also lift up Mr. Meany himself, as he struggles with his new dentures." See how spiritual "lifting up" sounds? And it's important to lift people up to God. That saves Him the trouble of having to stoop down and pick them up Himself.

We should attach one caveat to this tip. If you're praying for a person with Chronic Fatigue Syndrome, we suggest you leave out the lift-ups. After all, those with CFS probably don't want or need to be lifted up. Just let them lie down for a while and get some rest.

5. **Forget all of the above and be real.** We know this last tip is controversial. But maybe, just maybe, if you don't worry so much about impressing those around you and talk to your Father like a real person, you'll find that your prayers are more authentic and sincere, and all the performance anxiety will disappear because you're not performing anymore. You're praying. We like the prayer we heard a kid offer at a church picnic a while back: "Hey, God, like, thanks for this food and stuff. Except the cole slaw. And I want to tell You that I think You're really cool. Thanks again. Amen."

Even more terrifying than our church camp's giant mosquitoes was Lars, the ill-tempered, muscle-bound porridge chef.

The Night Chadd Caught on Fire for the Lord

L ike all good churches, Broomfield Baptist had a camp affiliation. Several members of our church sat on the board of Camp Je-I-Al-The-Wo-To-Me. This is short for "Jesus Is All the World to Me." The camp founders thought the shortened version sounded like a cool native saying. We thought it sounded like something you might scream if a weasel runs up your pant leg, but they didn't ask for our input.

However, they certainly did ask all the Hafer brothers to be camp counselors each summer. It was a task we dreaded. You see, Camp Je-Me (for the sake of even more brevity) wasn't one of those country club camps some of you may be used to. No mints on your pillows each night. No gourmet meals.

At this camp, "mess hall" was taken literally. Porridge was the staple food. After tasting this bland, paste-like concoction, we know why the three bears really left their house—they were afraid to eat the porridge. One night we snuck our bowls of porridge (porridge-'n-weenies, to be exact) to the lavatory and emptied them into the toilets. It clogged the entire septic system so badly that even Roto-Rooter had to radio for back-up. Yet the Je-Me staff expected us to eat this stuff.

And, yes, Camp Je-Me did have an obstacle course, but it wasn't one of those high-tech American Gladiators set-ups. The objective on this course was simple. You crawled on your belly through about a hundred yards of dry, prickly weeds, did ten chin-ups on an old rusty clothesline standard, then tried to cross the finish line. We say "tried" because the finish line was always guarded by Lars, the Porridge Chef. He would try to prevent you from completing the course by grabbing you in a full nelson and rubbing his stubbly chin on the back of your neck until you cried, "I submit to Lars the Great!" Lars took his obstacle-course duties seriously. He never smiled. We surmised that he was perpetually constipated from all the porridge he ate.

Camp Je-Me's most distinguishing characteristic, though, was its mosquitoes. Perhaps it was the moist mountain air that made them thrive. We don't know. But these weren't the whiney-tiny, annoying mosquitoes one typically encounters. These were bat-sized bloodsuckers with Cessna engines. When one of these rapier-nosed bugs bit you, he'd take so much blood that he'd give you a glass of orange juice and a sugar cookie afterwards.

So you can well imagine that our tours of duty at Camp Je-Me were not among the highlights of our summers. But we made the best of it. Every summer we brothers loaded up on allergy medicine and insect repellent and headed for camp.

We hoped and prayed that the days and nights would pass quickly and that Lars would lose his porridge recipe. And as we did every summer, we argued over who would have to speak at the fireside service on the final night of camp.

The fireside service was always held outdoors around a campfire for an emotionally ragged audience. After all, the kids had been tortured by Lars, attacked by the giant mosquitoes, and clogged with porridge sludge. Speaking at this service was like leading aerobics at an Anemics Anonymous Convention.

Speaking at this service was like leading aerobics at an Anemics Anonymous Convention.

At our final year of camp, Chadd lost the round-robin coin toss and was drafted into fireside duty. That was the year a camper spilled some porridge on his shirt. When the shirt was put into a washing machine, the laundry's plumbing system backed up like a debutante encountering a rattlesnake.

Thus, all of us had to make the best of limited wardrobes. This would prove devastating for Chadd. You see, the first night of camp a few of us became bored and decided to put underpants on the camp's canine mascots, Obadiah and Kimmie. Chadd's Jockeys just happened to be handiest.

Chadd enjoyed the sight of Obadiah and Kimmie frolicking about the camp in skivvies until we briefed him on the brief situation. He said, "Well, I'm not wearing those drawers again. I don't want to get distemper or something. Luckily, I still have three pairs left. I think I can make those last as long as I don't get dysentery."

Sadly on day two of camp, Chadd lost another pair of undergarments. Lars, in a surly mood after Chadd wriggled out of his full nelson and completed the obstacle course, took revenge that evening in mess hall. During the blessing, Lars snuck up behind Chadd and gave him an atomic wedgie. If you don't know what an atomic wedgie is, find any junior high kid in the country and ask him. Just don't ask him to demonstrate.

The, uh, bottom line to all this is that by the end of camp Chadd simply had no acceptable underwear. So as he stood by the campfire that final night, he was, as they say, "Going Commando."

None of us will ever forget Chadd's historic Camp Je-Me fireside chat. He stood near the fire in a "Wrestling Is Life" T-shirt and pair of 501 jeans— remember, the ones with the metal button-flies. We were amazed at his speech that night.

Usually a calm, even speaker, Chadd was impassioned. Sweat beaded on his forehead and upper lip. He seemed almost anguished as he encouraged the kids to "get their acts together and ignite with a burning passion to serve God." Toward the end of his message, his voice began to waver, and tears streamed down his reddening face.

"Wow," Jedd whispered to Bradd. "Chadd is really into this. I haven't seen him cry since they canceled *Charlie's Angels*."

What we didn't know was that Chadd wasn't crying tears of emotion or conviction. They were tears of pain. It's amazing what standing close to a fire can do to a set of metal buttons and rivets. They can get hotter than a Texas sidewalk in July. And without the usual protection of his genuine Jockeys, Chadd found himself truly on fire for the Lord. He was sobbing by the time he finished his prayer, at which point he ran to the creek and sat down in it. More than a few crayfish were steamed that night.

Chadd didn't endure the pain for nothing. The campers were so moved by his "riveting" speech that ten of them rededicated their lives. Even Lars vowed to be nicer and quit smoking, a habit he had entertained since age eleven. And we three other Hafer brothers made a commitment, too. We vowed that next time we would put someone else's underwear on the dogs.

None of us will ever forget that night—especially not Chadd. He has five circular "Levis" brands on his abdomen. Sometimes, these will get noticed when Chadd is at the swimming pool in his skimpy-yet-tasteful swimming trunks. "Dude," some kid will ask him, "like, what's the deal with those little Levi's tattoos?"

Chadd will smile and reply, "They were supposed to be Elvis tattoos, but the tattoo guy was dyslexic. Dude."

Chadd's fireside chat was the last ever at Camp Je-Me. When that summer ended, the board decided to invest its money in something more profitable, such as a Christian rock band or the stock market or South African Krugerrands.

Lars went on to become a professional wrestler by the name of The Porridge Mangler. Last we heard, he's undefeated.

The Theological Know-How Dudes, Part *Deux!*

This advice column is back by popular demand. Since our first installment of "The Theological Know-How Dudes," questions have literally been trickling in. And we believe that the tiny snowball of enthusiasm we've generated could turn into an avalanche any day now. Or not. We just like the snowball-avalanche comparison. Anyway, here are more of our careful answers to your burning questions.

Question: I'm deeply opposed to Earth Day. It seems pagan and New Age-like. What do you think?

Answer: Sorry to disagree, but we support Earth Day. After seeing many of our nation's leaders speak on TV, we think it's a good idea to have a yearly holiday that reminds everyone what planet we live on.

Question: Please settle a Sunday school argument. Was Zaccheus really the shortest man in the Bible?

Answer: No, li'l Zack was actually third shortest. The second shortest biblical figure was Knee-High Emia—a truly minor prophet. And the teensy crown for most diminutive Bible figure goes to the New

Testament Roman centurion who slept on his watch. You gotta be tiny to do that.

Follow up: That seemed like a long answer to such a short question. . . .

Question: In church last Sunday, our congregation sang a hymn about a cross-eyed bear named Gladly! I was appalled! What's next? Praise to Winnie the Pooh?

Answer: Uh, we think you might be a bit confused. Your congregation was probably singing "Gladly the Cross I'd Bear." Perhaps you missed the hymn's true meaning. Common mistake.

Question: How do you feel about women in the ministry?

Answer: What kind of incendiary question is that? Are you trying to get your lovable "Theological Know-How Dudes" in trouble? Let's just leave it at this. We think women are intelligent, capable, and mature people who can succeed wherever God leads them. Consider the National Basketball Association, which recently hired its first-ever women referees. These officials have done an incredible job. There's been only one noticeable difference between the women and their male counterparts. When a female ref calls a foul on a player, she also brings up all the fouls the player committed in the last three months.

Question: I'm contemplating attending Bible college. What do you think I should do?

Answer: You asked the right guys. We heartily encourage you to attend the Bible college or university of your choice—especially if that choice is Biola

University (because our Uncle Ron works there). You'll lay a firm foundation for your future. You'll be encouraged by the other young Christians preparing for a lifetime of service to the Lord. You'll grow in Christian knowledge. You'll meet godly friends. And when it's all said and done, you'll have a really cool tassel to hang from your rear-view mirror! One more suggestion: Major in communications, as we did. That way, after you graduate and are able to score a job bagging groceries, you'll be able to say, "Paper or plastic?" and really get your message across.

> We firmly believe that everything will pan out in the end.

Question: I'm confused about the "end times." Where do you guys stand? Are you premillennialists? Postmillennialists? Amillennialists?

Answer: We are panmillennialists. We firmly believe that everything will pan out in the end.

Question: Help! I'm trying to study the world's religions, but it's just so confusing. How can you keep all the religions straight?

Answer: We're happy to help you. We've devised an easy-to-recall overview using the popular expression, "Stuff Happens." We believe the best way to distinguish among world religions is to understand how they interpret this expression. So read on and learn:

A Brief "Stuff Happens" Overview of World Religions

Existentialism: Stuff happens, but what does it matter?

Hinduism: Hey, this stuff has happened before!

Extreme Islam: When stuff happens, take a hostage.

Zen: If stuff happens in the forest, does anyone hear it?

Buddhism: When stuff happens, is it really stuff?

Confucianism: Confucius say, "Stuff tend to happen."

7th-Day Adventism: Stuff happens, but never on Saturday.

Protestantism: Stuff won't happen if I just work harder.

Jehovah's Witness: Knock, knock. Stuff happens.

Presbyterianism: A sprinkle a day can keep stuff from happening.

Catholicism: If stuff happens, you probably deserved it.

Mormonism: Sorry that stuff happened on your nice suit, Oren.

Judaism: Oy! Why does this stuff keep happening to me?

Question: Have you two ever been told that you really have a gift?

Answer: Yes, we've been told we have a gift. But we've also been encouraged to return it.

Question: Would you two say that you have the fruit of the Spirit?

Answer: Well, sure, we have the fruit of the Spirit. It's just that ours isn't quite ripe yet.

Steve the Monk departed the Monastery
of General Ambiguity and headed for
no place in particular.

A Not-Too-Terrible Parable

Some of our favorite Bible passages are Jesus' parables. To us there is nothing like a parable to bring spiritual concepts to life. In fact, parables are so effective that we wonder why they are not used more today. We find this oversight disturbing. But Dad has always told us, "If you don't like the way things are, do something to change them. Or at least quit griping about it."

With those words echoing in our minds and hearts, we are attempting to revive the parable as a tool for imparting spiritual truth and wisdom. This is our first attempt, and we know it may not be New Testament quality. But give us a break; we're just a couple of prodigals with limited talent. Here we go . . .

The Parable of the Monk's Spiritual Quest

In a monastery perched on a high mountaintop, lived a devout monk named Steve. Steve spent every day fasting, meditating, and pondering all things spiritual.

But no matter how much he thought and meditated—or how little he ate—Steve could not find peace.

You see, his monastery wasn't a traditional one grounded in Scripture. It was called The Monastery of General Ambiguity, and it tended to inspire more questions than answers. Thus, Steve grew frustrated.

"What is the meaning of life?" he moaned to his fellow monks during one three-day fast.

"I don't know, Steve," one of his friends replied. "But I'd kill for a Twinkie right now."

After years of fruitless soul-searching, Steve finally gathered the courage to confront Stan, Head Monk at MGA. Quietly, he entered Stan's study.

"Most honorable Stan," Steve said humbly, "I have come to you with a question that has burned in my bosom for years."

Stan ceased his Thigh-Master exercises and wiped his forehead with the sleeve of his robe. "What is your question, my son?"

"What is the meaning of life? What is the purpose of it all?"

"Good one, Steve," Stan said. "That is what we in the higher planes of spirituality refer to as 'A Doozy of a Question.'"

"And I am in need of 'A Doozy of an Answer,'" Steve pleaded.

"Well, I suppose that life's purpose is to become one with everything."

"Ah, yes, Stan! That sounds like a worthy purpose! Please, can you make me one with everything?"

Stan sighed deeply and shook his head. "I'm sorry my son, I cannot. But I am up to 100 reps on my Thigh-Master! Wanna see?"

"No, thank you," Steve said quietly. "I fear that if you cannot help me fulfill my purpose in life, I shall collect my life savings and leave the monastery."

"As you wish," Stan said. He opened his desk drawer and carefully counted out all the money that Steve had entrusted to him when he joined MGA—three dollars and fifty cents.

Steve fled the monastery determined to find oneness with everything. As he descended the mountain, he came upon a philosopher sitting on a rock.

"Please, kind philosopher," Steve implored, "make me one with everything."

"What do I look like—a magician? I'm a philosopher!" the man snapped. "I have a degree in philosophy. I can't even get a job at a fast-food joint. Why do you think I sit on a stupid rock all day? By the way, could you lend me five bucks?"

"All I have is three dollars and fifty cents," Steve called over his shoulder as he hurried to the base of the mountain. There he found a magician. Remembering the unemployable philosopher's words, his heart leapt with hope.

> "Please, kind philosopher," Steve implored, "make me one with everything."

"Mister Magician," Steve began, "I beg you to use your magical powers and make me one with everything!"

The magician stroked his long gray goatee. "Hmm. Don't know that one. But I can pull an egg out of your ear! Wanna see?"

Nearly blinded by his tears of despair, Steve fled from the magician. He trudged despondently into town. The streets were deserted, save for a man in a hot dog stand. For no reason he could think of, Steve approached the hot dog vendor. He stood before him and cried out, "Please, make me one with everything! I beg of you!"

The vendor smiled broadly. "No problem," he told Steve. "That'll be three dollars and fifty cents!"

Another Not-Too-Terrible Parable

Wow. We have been stunned by the response to our efforts to revive the parable as a means of imparting spiritual truth. Our first effort (about Steve the Monk's spiritual quest) has elicited well under a million responses.

Thus, we are inspired to offer you yet another classic parable. This one is titled . . .

Vow-Wow-Wow

In a monastery perched on a mountaintop lived a devout monk named Steve (we know this is how the first parable began—we don't want to stray too far from our successful formula). However, this monastery differs from the first. This monastery, dubbed the Triple Whammy Monastery, required its inhabitants to take three vows: Chastity, Poverty, and Silence.

One fine Tuesday, a monk-hopeful named Bob decided to join up or enlist or whatever it is monk wannabes do. The head monk handed him a weathered sheet of parchment that explained the rules. No dating.

All worldly possessions must be donated to the church. And monks can speak only two words every seven years!

Bob whistled when he read the third requirement. Shocked, the other monks turned and stared at him. Bob panicked for a moment, then pointed to a chickadee perched on the monastery window. The monks nodded their heads in understanding.

Bob carefully tracked the days of his spiritual pilgrimage with a series of handsome wall calendars donated by the local community. His favorite was *From Mange to Kennel Cough: A Whole Year of Really Sick Dogs*. Through his keen attention to the passing of time, Bob knew the exact day when he had been in TWM for precisely seven years. On that day, he marched to the head monk's office. He entered, cleared his throat, and said, "Bed hard."

The next seven years crawled by like a wounded garter snake.

The head monk nodded his acknowledgment, then returned to his crossword puzzle.

Bob then charted his next seven years, aided by such calendars as *Street Mimes and the Burros They Occasionally Ride*. Then he strolled to the head monk's inner sanctum, moistened his lips, and uttered, "Food cold."

The head monk again nodded, then returned to his macrame.

The next seven years crawled by like a wounded garter snake. Even calendars like *Visiting Our National Parks With George "Goober" Lindsay* couldn't lift the bench-press bar of despair from Bob's chest.

But on the twenty-first anniversary of his entry to monkdom, Bob hobbled down to see the head monk. He let the last remnant of a breath mint dissolve in his mouth; then he spoke, "I quit."

The head monk slowly lifted his eyes from his "Where's Waldo?" cartoon. "I'm not surprised," he told Bob evenly. "You've been griping ever since you got here."

The Hare-Raising Ear Incident:
A Typical Hafer Family Car Trip

Our dad has always understood that a pastor's life can be hard on his family. That's why when we were kids, he'd load the family into our 1967 Chrysler Monstrosity and drive us to some remote spot for a little R&R. Most of you know R&R stands for rest and relaxation. For us it came to mean retribution and revenge.

You see, when you pack four brothers into the backseat of a car, conflicts over territorial boundaries and personal hygiene are going to emerge (e.g., "Stay on your own part of the seat, you stinky little twit!").

Dad handled our battles calmly. He never threatened to turn the Monstrosity around and go home. No one would have minded that. He merely sighed loudly every ten minutes or so and said, "I'll give you until the count of five to settle down back there, or I'm gonna have to get Old Testament on some behinds." The prospect of old-style biblical discipline usually settled the troubled waters for a few minutes. Unless of course, someone committed a major infraction, as Bradd did on one fateful trip.

We had stopped to visit our grandparents, who lived in a retirement community inhabited by 200 elderly people and about 2,000 rabbits. We have always loved the sight of the abundant bunnies frolicking everywhere, and we loved the prospect of catching one and making it our own. But on previous trips, we had been unsuccessful.

To our great surprise, Bradd, using knowledge he gleaned from Roadrunner cartoons, fashioned a crude trap that actually nabbed a fat black-and-white carrot chomper that we dubbed Mr. Spanky. To our even greater surprise, Mom and Dad agreed to let Mr. Spanky accompany us on the remainder of our trip. And most surprising of all, we were only a half mile from our grandparents' home when Mr. Spanky used the entire backseat as his own personal rest stop.

> We were only a half mile from our grandparents' home when Mr. Spanky used the entire backseat as his own personal rest stop.

"That's it, Mr. Spanky!" Chadd screamed. "You're stew meat!"

"It's not Mr. Spanky's fault," Bradd protested. "He just got excited and went wee, wee, wee all the way ho—."

"Excited?" Chadd countered. "I'm excited, too! But you don't see me wetting on everyone! Although, Bradd, maybe I should!"

"If we make the rabbit into stew, can I have his feet for luck?" Jedd asked.

Before things went too far, Dad stopped the car and freed Mr. Spanky who, feeling refreshed and jovial, hopped away in the direction of the retirement community.

Bradd wasn't the most popular person in the Monstrosity that day. All of us chided him mercilessly: "Hey, Bradd, maybe you can catch a skunk next time! Or how about a porcupine? They make great traveling companions!"

After enduring about fifteen minutes of this forceful rhetoric, Bradd snapped like a frozen toothpick, turning his wrath on Jedd, "Shut up, you puny germ! And move over! Your elbow is touching me!"

Perhaps crazed by the stench of rabbit wee-wee, Jedd fired back, "You move, Brer Rabbit! Better yet, why don't you get your soggy cottontail out of the car and hop off to live with your bunny friend!"

That did it. Bradd grabbed Jedd and started thumping him like a ripe cantaloupe. Jedd was in trouble. One of us should have intervened, but frankly, we were enjoying the fight too much. So a desperate Jedd resorted to the only defense he knew. He reached up, grabbed a handful of hair, pulled Bradd's earlobe close, and bit down—with Tyson-like ferocity.

Bradd ceased his pummeling and screamed first in agony, then in horror. "He bit my ear off. He bit my ear off! I can feel it dangling!"

Chadd and Todd pulled Bradd's hand away from his ear, wanting to see some carnage first-hand. Jedd sat silently, wondering what happened to the piece of Juicy Fruit gum he'd been chewing.

"Oh, no!" Bradd wailed. "My ear just dropped into my hand! You're toast, Jedd! An ear for an ear! An ear for an ear!"

Jedd jumped into the front seat and hid by Mom's feet. Dad pulled off the road and looked over the seat as Bradd slowly opened his hand to reveal a wet, grotesquely mutilated . . . wad of gum. It had stuck to Bradd's ear during the skirmish and actually protected him from the bite, which, we were disappointed to learn, barely left a mark.

We all laughed—even Bradd. But to this day, Jedd and Bradd aren't allowed to sit together in the backseat. Bradd has developed a deep admiration for Vincent Van Gogh, and Jedd has switched to Freedent gum because it won't stick to most parts of your head.

The Pastor's Wife:
Master of the Phone(y) Voice

As a pastor's wife, Sunday school teacher, Christian Women's Club speaker, and master VBS flannel-graph story teller, our mom has developed a voice as light, fluffy, and sweet as cotton candy. She makes Donna Reed sound like a chain-smoking truck driver.

However, a sweet voice doesn't cut the corn when disciplining kids—especially four free-spirited preacher's kids. So Mom also perfected a snarling, "Do you feel lucky, punks?" Dirty Harry voice that would scare a Marine drill sergeant out of his boots.

Mom usually reserved this harsh tone for when we had pushed her so far that she had but one nerve left, and we were jumping up and down on it.

Occasionally when Mom would be venting her wrath upon us, the phone would ring. We cherished these intermissions—not only because they kept us from being verbally filleted—but also because of the instant transformation they caused in Mom. Her scowl would disappear. Her brow would unfurrow. The tight jaw would relax. And that vicious snarl would become syrupy-sweet. It went something like this: "Listen up! If you little curtain-climbing monkeys don't straighten up right now, I'm gonna rip your . . . [ring-ring] . . .

helloooooooo and God bless you! This is Pastor Hafer's residence! How may I brighten your day?"

Get the picture?

We kids would just stand there, amazed. From Clint Eastwood to June Cleaver in one point two seconds. Even more incredible was the change back after the caller hung up. Immediately following her patented "Mmm-bye!" she shifted instantly back to her tirade: ". . . and another thing, you little stinkers— if I have to tell you to straighten up again, your worthless behinds are gonna be blue! How much of this do you think I'm gonna take?"

We weren't sure whether to answer. It could have been a rhetorical question. And we weren't sure whether to tremble or laugh at the contrast between "Phone-Mom" and "Psycho-Mom."

One day we learned that it's okay to laugh, but only if Mom laughs first. Mom was well into one of her classic bromides. She was nose-to-nose with Todd, to whom the punishment was delegated for the day. (It was usually impossible and woefully time consuming for Mom to determine which one of us instigated trouble, so we took turns bearing the brunt of parental wrath.)

"If that's how you're going to act," Mom threatened, "I'm going to stop doing anything for you! I'm through cooking. I'm through cleaning! I'm through doing laundry! From now on, you can all just, uh, fiend for yourselves!"

Now even as a child, Todd had an editor's mind. "Excuse me Mom, but I think you mean "fend." Fiend is not a verb," he said evenly.

Bradd chuckled nervously into the hollow silence. "Uh oh Mom. Looks like the editor-boy caught you," he said carefully. Then we waited.

Mom's neck-veins went back into hiding. The crimson drained from her face. She shook her head and laughed. Then she spoke to us in her sweet voice, "Oh, you boys, come here right now." She hugged each of us and apologized. We apologized, too.

In the months that followed, an interesting transformation took place. Since Mom could never yell at us again without one of us asking if we'd be required to "fiend for ourselves," she learned to properly channel her vocal rage by letting the telemarketers have it.

So please don't call her and ask if she's happy with her current long-distance carrier. Don't start extolling the benefits of aluminum siding. And don't—we beg of you—tell her she's won some lame contest. Because our mom will tear into you like an angry Doberman. Just like she did with the poor guy who recently tried to sell her a set of encyclopedias.

"Encyclopedias?" she screamed into the phone. "You think I can afford a whole set of encyclopedias? Well, Mister Salesman, let me clear up something for you. We're a poor preacher's family. But maybe I can afford just one volume. The one for the letter 'L'—for 'loser.' Let's look it up together, shall we? I bet we'll find your picture!"

Bet that poor salesman hung up feeling like a real fiend.

When Eunice, the 258-pound marimba player
from the Wesleyan Church, stepped to the plate,
everyone backed up. She had forearms
(and a goatee) like Mark McGwire.

Church Softball:
The Long Journey Home

Summer. Long, hot days. The smell of hot dogs. The ping of aluminum bats. Competitors from different denominations screaming, "Hey, tie goes to the runner, you dirty, uh, I mean my beloved sister in Christ!" Ah, yes, summer without church league softball would be like ping without pong, Christmas without a tree, Hootie without the Blowfish.

Every summer Dad would post a sign-up sheet in the church vestibule/foyer/narthex/lobby/fellowship area and encourage everyone to join the BBC Bombers in their quest for the coveted interdenominational pennant. Usually about thirty people signed up, including someone named Les Talented (our brother Chadd's pseudonym). When Saturday games rolled around, however, we were lucky if nine players showed up. Typically our dog, King, had to play "rover," which he found quite confusing.

All the churches loved softball season. The men players loved competing on a large grassy area that they didn't have to mow. And the women delighted in the opportunities to put their pseudo-macho husbands in their places—like "Rock," our mammoth catcher who has always told people that he is an ex-Marine who can "kill a dude just by using my thumbs."

Last season Rock's wife, Rockette, struck a deal with the pitcher from the Methodist team to throw Rock an inside fastball. Rock's eyes grew as big as pizzas, and he dove to the ground, squealing like a piglet. Rockette had to bribe him with brownies before he would uncurl from his fetal position and continue the game.

Our games were always filled with playful moments like this, but the real highlight is an incident that comes to mind from one of our post-season all-star games. Being chosen for the all-star game is a great honor. People in Broomfield crave it even more than one of those cornfield salutes from the cast of *Hee-Haw*. All-stars are carefully chosen for their skill, courage, determination, and sportspersonship. Being around in late August and not on summer vacation helps, too.

The latter criterion landed all four of the Hafer boys on the north all-star team last summer (north as in "north of the Dairy Delight"). Joining us on the squad were the finest non-vacationing players from the Catholic, Lutheran, Methodist, Full Gospel, and Deep-Southern Baptist churches. We reveled in our all-star status as we took the field for the first inning one scorching Saturday.

Unfortunately, the game quickly took an ugly turn. Our pitcher, "Hamster" Hampton, walked the first three batters, loading the bases. That set the table for Eunice, the 258-pound marimba player from the

Wesleyan Church, who smiled as she walked deliberately to the plate.

"Everybody back up!" Chadd called from left field. Chadd knew what Eunice could do with a bat in her hand. She hit twenty-four homers during the regular season, and she had forearms (and a goatee) like Mark McGwire.

Hamster tried to fool Eunice with a first pitch that was eyeball high and at least a foot outside. Eunice just glared at him and spit in the dirt. Hamster's next pitch, a fastball, was way inside, almost striking her elbow. Eunice intensified her glare. "Come on, Gerbil, gimme something to hit!" she chided.

> Our pitcher, "Hamster" Hampton, walked the first three batters, loading the bases. That set the table for Eunice, the 258-pound marimba player from the Wesleyan Church.

A word of advice: Don't call Hamster "Gerbil." He hates that. He maintains hamsters are ten times more intelligent, playful, and tidy than gerbils. He wrote his doctoral dissertation on the subject, and if he starts comparing and contrasting these two rodents you're in for a long day. So Eunice's insult cut Hamster right to his little hamster wheel of a heart. He blinked the tears from his eyes and whipped a fastball to Eunice right in the middle of the strike zone.

The smack of Eunice's bat on that softball reminded us of the sound of the spankings Chadd received when he was twelve. Bradd drifted back to the deepest part of center field and studied the ball's skyscraping trajectory.

On a normal day, Eunice's ball would have cleared the field and landed into the McGintys' hot tub. But the wind was blowing in on all-star Saturday. So Bradd, his back pressed against the McGintys' fence, leaped high (well, as high as a Hafer brother can leap), and snagged the ball on the first bounce.

Then he switched the ball from his glove to his right hand and squinted his eyes. He saw Eunice still waddling to first base. You see, Eunice, while powerful, is slow and ungainly—much like a Senate subcommittee. So Bradd rared back and launched a throw to first base. Eunice's foot plopped on the bag just as the ball struck her on the forehead. She hit the ground like a British heavyweight.

Both teams ran to first base and stood over Eunice, who was moaning, "Oh, Mommy! Oh, Mommy!"

"Quick!" hollered the Assembly of God all-stars. "Let's lay hands on her!"

"No," countered Pete the Presbyterian, "we need to sprinkle her with pure water—or Gatorade."

"You're on the right track, Pete," said Micah, a utility infielder from the Deep-Southern Baptists. "But for maximum healing power, she must be submerged."

The Episcopalians wanted to anoint Eunice with oil. The Catholics offered to say some Hail Mary's, but Hamster argued that those were to be used only in football.

Meanwhile, Eunice was still doing her mommy chant and flopping on the ground like a just-caught catfish.

Since consensus couldn't be reached on a healing method, all of the various team members began applying their respective practices to poor Eunice. She was the most prayed-over (and the wettest) athlete in all of Broomfield. She's just lucky the Deep-Southern Baptists couldn't find anything bigger than an empty Big Gulp cup.

Then, everyone stood back and watched. Eunice stopped wailing and began to finger her forehead gingerly, wincing as she touched the egg-sized lump the softball had created. "I'm okay," she said, rising slowly to her feet. "And, by the way, I was safe."

No one was going to argue that call.

"Hurray!" called Pete the Presbyterian. "The sprinkling worked!"

"Nah, it was the oil," the Episcopalians contended.

A vicious debate ensued, each denomination claiming credit for Eunice's recovery.

Just as it looked like the Interdenominational All-Star game would turn into a World Wrestling Federation free-for-all, Eunice's daughter, Eunice Jr., pushed through the throng. She hugged her mom's leg for a moment, then turned to the crowd. "Maybe it wasn't any of you," she said. "Maybe it was God."

The outcome of that high-spirited all-star game is still in question. We think that we, the north-of-Dairy-Delight Christians, might have prevailed, but we just can't recall for sure. However, the words of little Eunice Jr. still ring clearly in our minds.

Up and Adam

Adam is one of our favorite Bible characters for several reasons. He was always a shoo-in for *Who's Who*. He never had a mother-in-law. He didn't have to worry about other guys trying to steal his girl. The toilet seat being up was never an issue. And he never had to hear those fateful words, "Why can't you be more like _____?"

But most of all, we like Adam because he was—and this isn't widely known—the world's first comedian. In fact he invented the joke. One day, Eve asked him, "Adam, do you love me?"

He shrugged his bare shoulders and said, "Who else?"

We'd like to introduce you to Adam, the world's pioneer humorist, as he goes about his daily activities in Eden. Look, there he is sneaking up behind Eve and putting his hands over her eyes:

"Guess who-ooooo?"

"Oh, Adam, you are so silly!"

"Ah, you guessed right again! You're pretty smart for someone made from a rib!"

"Let's not go there, dust-boy!"

"Touché, Eve. Hey, I've been meaning to ask you something. If we decide to have kids and one of them is a boy, can we name him Abel?"

"Abel? What kind of name is that? It's rather sheepish. And then I suppose we'll have to name his siblings Ready and Willing? Nuh-uh. Especially not if they're girls. I kind of prefer Cain as a boy's name."

"Cain? Oh, spare me. That rhymes with pain. A boy named Cain is gonna be nothing but trouble, Eve."

> "Cain? Oh, spare me. That rhymes with pain. A boy named Cain is gonna be nothing but trouble, Eve."

"Let's just not discuss it right now, Adam. Let's talk about something else. Like what you are wearing."

"But I'm wearing nothing."

"Precisely. And nothing is so, so . . . last season. I'm bored with both our wardrobes."

"So you're complaining that you have nothing to wear?"

"Precisely. Maybe we should try putting on some fig leaves for a change."

"Eve are you kidding? Wear those itchy, scratchy fig leaves on our bodies? I'll tell you something; I wouldn't be caught dead walking out of this garden wearing fig leaves!"

"Whatever you say, Adam. You know, all this arguing is making me hungry. Let's go down by the peach tree and have some dinner."

"That's a great idea, honey. You know how I love peaches. You are so thoughtful! There's just no other woman in the world for me."

"You can say that again, Adam."

"And after dinner, we can go for a walk into the center of the garden."

"I don't know, Adam. That serpent likes to hang out down there. He creeps me out."

"Ah, Eve, relax. What harm can a little snake do?"

One blizzardy Sunday, the snowplow driver got the flu. So, armed with one snow shovel, one army shovel, a dustpan, and exactly five gloves for four boys, we began to remove the mountainous drifts from the church parking lot.

The Preacher's Kids
Will Do It

Sometimes we Hafer boys thought our parents brought us into the world as a means of cheap labor. We expressed this opinion, to which Dad would reply, "Your accusation is false and hurtful. Your mom and I had you kids because we feel that the world needs children to remind it of how fragile, innocent, and beautiful life is. Now go clean the garage."

Yes siree! Our parents were determined to teach us that hard work and diligence pay off in the long run. (Although it must be said that laziness always pays off right now!) Anyway, the reason we sometimes saw ourselves as mere beasts of burden is that whenever anyone in the church needed a dirty job done, Dad got the call and happily volunteered us. Then he would try to frame our duty in the most positive terms, but we quickly learned to break his code:

"Fellas, I have a little project for you." (Translation: This is going to consume every waking hour of your day.)

"A little lady in the church needs her lawn mowed and a few weeds and stuff cleared." (Translation: A little lady with a lawn the size of the Ponderosa and overrun with ten-foot jungle weeds wants you to mow her lawn with a rusty three-quarter horsepower mower with two missing wheels. But you will be expected to give her spread the well-manicured look of the infield at Yankee Stadium.)

"She is fairly well-to-do, so she'll probably take care of you guys pretty well. This could be lucrative." (Translation: She is loaded, but she keeps her money in a pair of panty hose that she hid someplace in 1953. She's not sure where that place is, so at the end of three days of hard labor at the peak of allergy season she'll slip you each a quarter and a warm glass of Tang.)

"But, Dad," we'd protest, "this sounds like a big job. Can't you come and help us?"

"I'm sorry, but I can't guys. I have to stay here and study for my sermon." (Translation: "I'm gonna stay here and fall asleep in my big, comfortable recliner.")

So we would trudge out of the house to embark on some labor that belonged in a Greek tragedy.

One blizzardy Sunday, the snowplow guy who always cleared the church parking lot had the flu. So armed with one snow shovel, one army shovel, a dustpan, and exactly five gloves for four boys, we began to remove the mountainous drifts from the parking lot.

There was so much snow that we weren't even sure where the parking lot was. And when our eyelids began to freeze shut—well, that made the whole thing that much more unpleasant. Adding to our displeasure was Jedd's constant whining that he should get to wear at least one of the gloves. Sometimes little kids can be so picky.

Fortunately on this day, the preacher's kids got a reprieve. An off-duty policeman driving a Snow-cat rumbled by. "Hey, fellers," he called. "Go home. All the roads in town are closed. Only a bunch of boneheads would be out on a day like this!"

We fought our way through the snow back to the house, where we found Dad, snoring away in his large, comfortable recliner. We thought about waking him up and giving him what-for for sending us out into the Arctic-like tundra to toil away while he slept in the warm house. But we held our tongues. We knew what he'd say: "How many times have I told you kids not to interrupt me when I'm . . . uh . . . meditating?"

When our eyelids began to freeze shut—well, that made the whole thing that much more unpleasant.

But don't think we lack assertiveness. Now that we're grown up, we're better able to resist Dad's efforts to con us into dirty, backbreaking jobs. We'd love to expound on this subject, but it's Sunday afternoon and time to go help Dad collect 632 tiny plastic communion cups and wash them with a couple of toothbrushes.

Pondering Fame and Fortune

"**Y**ou know, Jedd and Todd, if your book does well, your lives are going to change. But you better not change."

We weighed these words carefully because they came from a guy named Dirk, whom we respect for his wisdom—and for the fact that he's the size of a major appliance and as strong as a gorilla. Dirk was a high school football star from Texas. As you enter his hometown (we'll call it Hornetville), you are greeted by a sign that says:

WELCOME TO THE HOME OF THE CLASS AA
STATE FOOTBALL CHAMPS
1963, 1968, 1979, 1982

not

WELCOME TO HORNETVILLE—OUR KIDS
KNOW HOW TO READ!

Nope, in Dirk's town, like many in rural America, community pride rests on the broad, armored shoulders of high school football players.

Dirk responded well to the pressure. As strong and fast as he is big, he was all-state in high school. He went on to play college ball for the University of New Mexico. You know New Mexico, don't you? It's where they film most of the Roadrunner cartoons.

After a successful college career, Dirk made it to the NFL. Not as a big star; you probably wouldn't recognize his name (even if we hadn't changed it), but enough to make him a legend in Hornetville and surrounding areas. He can get free food at any place in town. And if he accidentally runs over an armadillo in his sports car, the local authorities look the other way.

> He can get free food at any place in town. And if he accidentally runs over an armadillo in his sports car, the local authorities look the other way.

But the success and preferential treatment haven't gone to Dirk's pumpkin-sized head. He isn't cocky. He doesn't do drugs. And even though he's reduced many a fullback to a mere crimson stain on the turf, he hugs kids and takes care not to crush your carpals and metacarpals when he shakes your hand. He's also generous. He always tips well, whether it's a waitress or a shoe-shine guy in an airport. (And those shoe-shine guys earn their money with Dirk. His feet look like pieces of living-room furniture.)

Dirk finds it ironic that people are genuinely surprised when a successful actor, musician, or athlete is kind and cordial to them. "Why shouldn't we be nice?" he asked us. "We have maids, limo drivers, personal assistants, agents, and publicists all helping us out. Why do so many celebrities refuse to sign an autograph for a kid while some janitor with seven mouths to feed and a car that doesn't run right will offer to buy you a cup of coffee or lend you his lawn mower?

"Remember the winter Olympics a while back? The criminal American skater whined about her shoe-lace while the thirteen-year-old Ukrainian war orphan skated with a smile. I hope you guys will be like her—just happy to have a chance to do your thing."

We nodded at Dirk and pledged to remember his words.

So if this book is successful, we promise that we'll pet dogs, build playgrounds, and occasionally walk into the local pizza parlor and buy pie for everybody—bread sticks, too. And if we ever start wearing something other than athletic shoes, we'll tip shoe-shine professionals generously and graciously.

There it is in writing. We're accountable to you now. So if you ever catch us acting like spoiled jerks, tell us to knock it off. Or, better yet, call Dirk, a guy whose heart will always be bigger than his wallet. He'll put us in our places right away.

Church:
Getting There Isn't Half the Fun

We miss the days when we lived in the parsonage right next to Broomfield Baptist Church. Getting to church was much simpler then. The biggest obstacles were mud puddles or an occasional dead squirrel on the sidewalk. Both could be leaped in a single bound.

Now that we have our own homes and live farther from church, things are different. We have to get on the highway to get to church. And getting on the highways in Colorado is a risk tantamount to bungee jumping with a cord made of old tube socks.

People in Colorado have an unusual philosophy about driving. For example, if you are driving a vehicle that looks like the Mystery Machine from *Scooby Doo*, you should occupy the highway's left lane and proceed at funeral-procession speed. If you can find an RV in the right lane and drive perfectly parallel with it, so much the better.

Furthermore if you use your turn signal in most states, it means you plan to turn. In Colorado, using your blinkers is a sign of weakness. Or at least bad strategy. It's like playing for the Denver Broncos and letting the Raiders into your huddle. "Why should we signal?" Colorado drivers ask angrily. "That would only tip off the enemy (e.g., other drivers) to our plan. Then they might not have to screech to a stop when we suddenly decide to turn or switch lanes, depriving us of the opportunity to scream and make obscene gestures at them."

Thus, we do as much praying in the car on the way to church as we do once we're safely inside the sanctuary. And we must confess that the death-defying drive to church is getting to us.

In Colorado, using your blinkers is a sign of weakness. Or at least bad strategy. It's like playing for the Denver Broncos and letting the Raiders into your huddle.

One recent Sunday was particularly harrowing. Our families were driving to church together in our Mitsubishi Montero. We had already avoided five stealth lane-changers and a speeding elderly woman in a Ford Festiva who apparently learned to navigate her vehicle at the Kelsey Grammer Driving School.

Then as we approached the exit for church, we saw a pickup truck just ahead of us with an I HATE TEXAS bumper sticker overshoot the same exit. So the truck pilot did what any good Colorado driver would do: He skidded to a stop and backed up on the highway until he was able to make the exit. Actually, he appeared to be pretty saavy in that he knocked over only one reflector pole in the process.

Seeing the pickup's rear end speeding toward us almost made our nerves snap like old rubber bands. As we reached the stoplight at the end of the exit ramp, we were as mad as turnips. (And if you don't think turnips can be angry, think of the heartburn they can cause.) Stopped at the light ahead of us, however, was something that calmed our troubled spirits. It was a yellow Gremlin with a tattered bumper sticker with sky-blue letters. It said: VISUALIZE WORLD PEACE.

That sticker gave us pause. All of us in the Montero decided that was exactly what we needed—to visualize peace. So we all closed our eyes, quieted our minds and hearts, and pictured a peaceful meadow. Birds chirping softly. Grass blades bending gently in the warm breeze. Clouds floating by overhead, offering protection from the searing sun. We visualized children of all ages and races frolicking together and singing songs in perfect four-part harmony. We pictured lambs and wolves drinking side by side at a lush oasis, then curling up together for a refreshing nap. We heard the healing sounds of . . .

HONK! HONK! HONK-HONKETY-HONK HOOOOOOOONNNNNNNNNNK!

The horn of an angry motorist behind us robbed us of our bliss. We opened our eyes to see that the light was green. And the Gremlin, with its message of peace, was gone. But we weren't about to give up on that message. So for the sake of world peace, we had to get out of the car and deflate the tires of a beet-red

Cadillac from Texas. We bet that's the last time those Shriners interrupt other motorists' meditations. Especially since we took one of their fezzes and flattened it.

Our little exercise in retribution made us five minutes late for church, but sometimes that's the price you have to pay for world peace.

The Late Misters Hafer

To be a Hafer male is to be late. Dad, AKA the Late Reverend Del Hafer (he's alive, just never on time), has passed the tardiness curse on to his sons. When we say "curse," we aren't trying to evade responsibility. It's just not our fault.

Whenever a Hafer male is trying to get someplace, all of the forces of technology, humanity, and nature conspire against him to halt his progress. Buttons break. Zippers stick. Keys hide. Traffic jams. Meanwhile, time itself speeds up. We dislike this phenomenon, but we've learned to accept it.

There's only one problem. Our parents—especially Dad—have always been understanding when we're late for dinner, funerals, ball games, weddings, and yacht christenings. But we've never been allowed to be late for church. In fact, being late to church carried a double penalty. First, we would cringe under the glare of Mom and Dad's disapproving looks. Then, once we got home, we'd be swatted like dusty throw rugs. (Incidentally, Dusty Throwrugs is our favorite country singer.)

Being late to church carried a double penalty. First, we would cringe under the glare of Mom and Dad's disapproving looks. Then, once we got home, we'd be swatted like dusty throw rugs.

Anyway as a matter of survival, we had to learn to slip into church unnoticed on those inevitable occasions when the church bell rang out eleven o'clock and we were still looking for a right shoe, left sock, or clean shirt. And once we arrived late, we couldn't merely hang out in the narthex, because Chet the elder patrolled the narthex like a well-trained German Shepherd. If he caught folks loitering back there, he'd gently remind them, "There's plenty of pew space up front." If said people continued to loiter, Chet wasn't above slapping them into a hammer-lock and personally escorting them to those pews with a view.

Thus, we each devised methods of foiling Chet and our parents. Perhaps you are a chronic late-arriver, as we are. Or perhaps you are consistently punctual, yet dread the day when you are tardy and have to face the shame of walking in late. Whatever the case, we now offer the Hafer brothers' patented approaches to slipping into church virtually unnoticed.

Bradd's Method

After ingesting your fourth bowl of Lucky Charms (and hiding the toy surprise from your brothers), you exit the house and head to church. Once there, you select a non-squeaky door and slip inside. Next, look for an usher, preferably a gullible one. Approach him, tap him on the shoulder, and inform him that while you are not 100 percent certain you think you saw his car on fire in the parking lot. Offer to hold his offering plate while he goes outside and checks.

If you time it just right, the usher/sucker will be looking for a blazing car while you march to the front of the auditorium with the other ushers to take the offering. After you have completed your duty, you can sit proudly wherever you like.

Really important note: If you decide to use the Bradd method, remember never to approach the same usher twice.

Todd's Method

Diversion is the key to this tactic. The individual using this method (we'll call him Todd) enters the church from downstairs (that's where Broomfield houses its nursery and junior church services), goes directly to the nursery, and asks to borrow a large, lifelike doll, saying the junior church leader needs to use it as an illustration. Then wrap the doll in a blanket, place it against your shoulder, and walk upstairs to the narthex. Once in the narthex, gently rock from one foot to the other, patting the doll on its plastic back. For the sake of authenticity, occasionally coo, "It's okay, Mookie. Your Uncle Todd has you. Don't you cry."

If you use Todd's method, you can loiter in the narthex indefinitely because not even Chet the elder would attempt to put an infant in a hammer-lock.

Really important note: Remember never to ask Chet to take the baby for a few minutes while you take a restroom break.

Jedd's Method

This method is simple. Upon entering the church, find the person running the sound equipment and slip in next to him or her. (At BBC it's Eddie from Radio Shack.) Slip the sound technician a five-spot (or in Eddie's case some Star Trek memorabilia) in exchange for co-piloting the sound system. Then as people are exiting the sanctuary after church, give Eddie (or whomever) a big hug and say loudly enough for everyone to hear, "I'm glad I could help you out with those bass levers! I think we've got a bad woofer, though. Better get it checked out!"

Chadd's Method

For the sake of full disclosure, we acknowledge that few people other than Chadd can pull this one off. Chadd typically arrives at church ten or fifteen minutes late, and then strolls brazenly down the center aisle and sits in the front pew. When Dad shoots him an accusing glare, Chadd merely winks at him and discreetly gives him the "zip-up-your-fly" sign.

After church Dad actually thanks Chadd. "Appreciated the zipper tip, pal. I didn't even realize it was down."

"No problem, Dad," Chadd will say. "What's a son for?"

Eating the Widow Larson's shingles was
bad enough. But when Manny Goat began
to devour her decorative rooster weather vane,
we knew immediate action was in order.

Getting the Pastor's Goat (Off the Roof!)

Our family wasn't rich even though Mom worked outside the home and Dad usually held one or two part-time jobs in addition to pastoring. One reason for our steadfast reign in Lower Middle Class Land was that Dad often accepted alternate forms of currency for his work.

Patrons on his milk route soon learned that a cherry pie or plate of brownies was just as good as a check made out to Watts-Hardy Dairy, Inc. And Dad would gladly split a cord of wood in exchange for an office chair covered in faux pea-green leather.

But the most unusual barter Dad ever made came after he helped Old Man O'Makowsky stack hay one sauna-like Saturday afternoon. "Thanks for your help, Pastor," O'Makowsky said when the work was done. "But I'll have to owe you the money . . . less'n you see something around here you want?"

A comment like that to our dad is like turning a monkey loose in a banana tree. And so it came to pass that Dad came home that day with a goat in his school bus. (Bus driver was another of his part-time gigs.)

We'll never forget the sight of Dad pulling the goat down the bus steps. Its eye bugged out as if it were being strangled. Its long white beard encrusted with . . . well, perhaps it was lemon yogurt. If not, we don't want to think about it. And when the goat bleated, it sounded like Katherine Hepburn singing "Memories" while reclining on a Magic Fingers vibrating bed.

And the smell. Ah, yes, the smell. In case you've never had the exquisite opportunity to sniff a goat, imagine the stench of a Porta-Potty at a monster truck rally. Then imagine something worse—far worse. That's how bad a goat stinks.

"Ah, Dad," Chadd whined. "Couldn't you have gotten a pie? Even some store-bought donuts would have been better than this."

"Come on, kids," Dad pleaded. "Give Nanny here a chance. Goats are actually very intelligent, and I've always loved goat's milk. Let me tell you once you've tasted goat's milk you'll think cow's milk is for the birds. Now somebody go in and get me a bucket so I can milk good ol' Nanny."

Someone fetched Dad a bucket, then we all went into the house because Nanny's B.O. (or G.O.) was stinging our eyes.

About fifteen minutes later, Dad limped inside. His shins were bruised and raw. And he had a large knot in the middle of his forehead where Nanny had butted him. He shook his head sadly. "Either Nanny is really dehydrated," he sighed, "or she's a boy."

After we all ran outside to examine our pet, the family voted 5-0 (with one abstention) that Nanny was indeed Manny. We took some rope and tied him to the clothesline and walked toward the house, fearing that we might never taste fresh goat's milk.

Several minutes later, we got a call from Gretchen, the church secretary.

"Pastor Hafer," she screamed, "I'm next door in the church office, and I'm hearing terrible noises up on the roof! Do you think the Antichrist is up there? Could this be Armageddon? Please go outside and check! I'm going to hide under my desk now."

Dad bounded out the door— the four of us right on his heels. The first thing we noticed was that Manny had chewed through the rope and partially eaten a pair of Dad's work pants and a few of Mom's unmentionables.

After we all ran outside to examine our pet, the family voted 5-0 (with one abstention) that Nanny was indeed Manny.

We heard a dull ringing sound atop the church and looked heavenward to see Manny head-butting the church bell. Then apparently bored, Manny ran down the church roof and leaped onto the roof of the Widow Larson's house. There he proceeded to eat her shingles, pausing briefly to take a bite out of her decorative rooster weather vane.

By this time, quite a crowd had gathered. All eyes were on Dad as he tried to coax Manny down from Mrs. Larson's roof. Dad tried everything. Pleading. Shouting. Reverse psychology. But Manny paid no attention. He just kept eating shingles and occasionally bleating "Memories" at the top of his great goat lungs.

Various people brought fresh vegetables with which to entice Manny. But he turned up his filthy chin at a fresh ear of supermarket corn and rolled his bulging eyes at a prize carrot from Mrs. Wedermeyer's garden.

It appeared that Manny had "gotten our goat" until Jedd had a burst of inspiration. After contemplating Manny's disgusting personal habits, he ran into the house and returned with a dirty gym sock filled with horseradish. Manny was off the roof and munching on that sock in a New York minute. Amazingly, eating the sock actually seemed to improve Manny's breath.

Mom told Dad that either she or Manny would be leaving the family that night, so Dad decided to donate Manny to the Methodists, who always used live animals in their nativity scenes. Sadly, as Christmas drew nigh and the Methodists went through their first nativity "dry run," Manny butted the Virgin Mary, gnawed a wise man's silk bathrobe, and chewed the right arm completely off of the plastic baby Jesus.

The Methodists are gentle folk, but Manny had clearly crossed the line. We don't want to go into detail about his punishment, but we can sum it up in two words: goat sausage.

There are two important lessons to be learned from Manny's saga. First, there's a reason we don't use the barter system anymore. Second, the next time you feel people are trying to "get your goat," by all means let them!

Just Say "No" to That New Age Nonsense

When we were growing up, our Mom and Dad were known as folks who stood up for "right." That deep sense of responsibility has been passed along to all of us, regardless of what line of work we have chosen for our lives. That's why Jedd and I decided that we must use this forum to unveil a devious deception that has somehow slipped below the radar screen of many Christians. And no, we don't mean the Spice Girls.

We are talking about the New Age Movement (or NAM). Sure, Christians used to care about NAM. Books and articles were published. Radio commentators warned Christians of the dangers. Pastors took to the pulpit to caution their congregations about evil NAM proponents. But somehow this once front-burner danger moved to the back burner, then tumbled from the stovetop entirely. It's lying there on your kitchen floor right now behind your GE or Kenmore or whatever, covered with cobwebs and dead earwigs. But it's only dormant, not dead. It is gathering strength and waiting till the time is right to harmonically converge on your home and turn all its inhabitants into crystal gazing, "om"-chanting, Maharishi-channeling new agers!

To this evil plot, we must say "enough!" Although many Christians have ignored NAM in favor of more trendy dangers (such as Olestra and the Disney Corporation), the fact remains that the movement is alive and well in our world, and it will continue to reincarnate itself until it has sucked every Christian into its pseudo-blissful vortex. (Please forgive us for that last term, but we bet some guys on our church softball team that we could get the words "pseudo-blissful vortex" into a book. And now they owe us a dozen donuts! Pay up, losers!")

Anyway, we're here to remind you about the size, scope, and danger of NAM. Shirley you must—we mean—surely you must agree that it's time to cease ignoring this problem.

For those who are unfamiliar with NAM, allow us to enlighten you. And we mean enlighten in its most Christian definition. It's estimated that NAM rakes in about forty billion dollars a year. This is a sizable sum given that NAM spends very little money on overhead items, such as office supplies. Since new agers believe they can "channel" messages from one member to another, they pay no more than eight thousand dollars a year for personalized stationery, faxes, memo pads, and staples.

Further, NAM's corporate headquarters occupy only three rooms of an office building that also contains a dog grooming salon, an electrolysis clinic, and a modern dance studio. But from this humble nerve center, NAM is responsible for polluting the minds and spirits of the world with well-disguised propaganda, awful movies, and vile pan-flute music. Members of NAM have also been known to smuggle bean curd across state lines for illegal experimental purposes. What's more, new agers often help other heretical groups accomplish their agendas by lending them umbrellas on rainy days, holding their coats, or baking them tofu cookies.

The tentacles of this empire extend even to the highest levels of government. NAM leaders have been spotted playing squash or Jenga with U.S. senators. And it's rumored that after partying with our nation's leaders they are even welcome to sleep on the sofa at the White House when they've had too much lemon grass tea to attempt driving home.

How did this glassy-eyed group gain such influence? We're glad we asked that rhetorical question. In the U.S., NAM really got off the ground (pardon the expression) in 1918 when Sheree "Moonbeam" Mendinkins and her quilting bee began experimenting with altered states of consciousness. Sometimes they would sniff freshly opened packages of burlap until they began to feel, as Sheree later described in her memoirs, "loopy."

On other occasions, Sheree would lock her quilting gang in a closet, lie on the floor outside, and attempt to suck the oxygen out of the closet with a straw. After months of being subjected to this treatment, several members of Sheree's bee did irrational things like selling all their belongings and going to live with yaks on mountaintops or running for city government.

In the late twenties, Sheree teamed with "Bad" Aura Rizing and began to market healing crystals and herbal tea under the name Sealed with a Bliss. These two women are also responsible for starting the trend of dotting i's with little hearts and coining the phrases "Reincarnate this!" and "Get a life—or twelve!"

NAM is organized like many businesses, corrupt third world governments, and organized crime families. At the top of the mountain is the Crestono de Tutti Capi or "Flake of all flakes." NAM meetings are usually held at this person's home or apartment, and he or she is usually responsible for providing granola, tofu-based cold cuts, and ice cubes for all meetings. Failure to do so is punishable by death which, given new agers' belief in reincarnation, is a penalty viewed as less severe than having to do twenty push-ups or paying a twenty-five-dollar fine.

Under the main Flake are Tutti des Blopo or "Flakes off the ol' flake." Each of these lieutenants is responsible for a certain area of New Age influence—such as lobbying to get Dan Rather to use the word "karma" at least once in his nightly newscasts. Recruiting for NAM is also a major responsibility and is achieved through stuffing leaflets under people's windshield wipers, late-night infomercials, and booths at craft fairs.

Initiation into NAM is a complex and closely guarded secret. Each NAM hopeful is blindfolded and led into a deserted part of North Dakota known as "North Dakota." Then eight sweet pickles are placed into each of the inductee's pants pockets, and he or she is required to hop up and down chanting, "Enya never perspires, by golly-golly-goo!"

Following this, individuals are forced to sit on a freshly cut crystal for ten minutes. All complainers are disqualified. Those who smile and say, "A crystal is a spanking-good chair!" are welcomed into the organization. This is usually done by kissing them on the cheek and sprinkling oat bran in their hair.

In summary, the New Age Movement is a large pimple on the face of our nation. Each year scores of America's youth are enticed by NAM's hollow promises of inner peace and an easy life. In reality most new agers work long hours cutting crystals and weaving pot holders from the hair of their own beards. (This is especially hard on the women.) What's worse is that this work is usually done in buildings with poor ventilation and no air conditioning.

So beware.

We believe that these are the best ways to protect yourself and your loved ones from the New Age Movement:

- Avoid any used bookstore that contains a juice bar and a man in a robe sitting cross-legged and playing the sitar.

- If a new age recruiter calls your home, don't give him a chance to start proselytizing. Immediately inform him that you represent the long-distance phone service known as "Ten-ten-eleven-456-Hut one, Hut two, Hike!" and ask him if he'd like to switch carriers.

We hate skiing because it combines
two of our least favorite things:
pain and cold.

Have Skis, Will Fall

Our church has an unusual tradition that we hate almost as much as the "Annual All-Church Weekend of Fellowship, Cleaning Out the Rain Gutters, and Ridding the Pew Bottoms of Gum Event."

The dreaded tradition of which we speak is the "Get-Closer-to-God Ski Weekend." We hate everything about it. We hate piling into rented buses at 5:00 A.M., loading up on donuts and convenience-store coffee, and settling in for a three-hour ride to a ski resort. The ride seems nearly twice as long given that we have to participate in the endless sing-along of "ninety-nine Cartons of Milk on the Wall." Also, we have to hear eighty-five variations of the question, "Dude, when we, like, get to the mountain, can I, like, borrow your sun screen?"

Then when we get to the ski village, we are forced to dine in one of those fancy ski resort restaurants. "It's all part of the ski experience," the "Get Closer to God" veterans tell us.

In case you've never been to one of these highbrow eateries, let us share our pain with you. First, the wait staff are bedecked in tar-black pants, stiffly

starched white shirts with ruffly sleeves, and red bow-
ties. Plus none of them have normal names. It's all
Fondette, Jade Sky, Marco-Marco, and Esteban Puy-Puy.

Once you are seated, these oddly monikered
people begin to deluge you with information, perhaps
to compensate for the expensive prices: "Hi, my name
is Berlin. My father is an investment banker, and my
mother makes potholders from the manes of Shetland
ponies. I shall be your server for brunch this morning.
Before I get to the specials, I would like to note that I
weigh one hundred five and one-half pounds and have
been on Acutane for three months. Please note my
skin's healthy hue."

And if you think this is a truckload of information,
wait until Berlin gets to the menu: "Our special today
is pan-blackened free-range chicken, prepared by
Hans, a six-foot-two, one hundred and ninety-pound
former javelin thrower from Liechtenstein. By the way,
tonight's chickens are named Afredo, Eduardo, and
Skylar-Moon."

Not surprisingly, such haute cuisine doesn't sit well
in the stomachs of the Brothers Hafer, guys whose idea
of a gourmet meal is putting Grey Poupon mustard on
foot-long hot dogs. The resort fare never fails to create
a gas bubble or two in our blue-collar stomachs.

Unfortunately, what would be a harmless little gas
bubble in Colorado's foothills becomes something else
in the high altitude of a ski resort. In other words,
what would make us mildly uncomfortable in
Broomfield makes us parade floats in Aspen. ("Look,
Kathie Lee, following the Underdog float are the

Flying Bloated Hafer Brothers. And don't they look unhappy. I guess that goose liver pate with lemon grass isn't sitting well!")

The worst part of the church ski weekend, though, is the skiing. You see, though we are Colorado natives, we are not big skiers. However, before you denounce us as traitors to our state and begin to pelt us with snowballs, please let us explain.

We know we are in the wrong. We know that we are not living up to our Colorado citizenship requirements. We know we're supposed to have four-wheel drives that cost more than our houses—and they're supposed to have several native bumper stickers and at least one anti-Texas sticker per vehicle as well. We know we should have ridiculously expensive sunglasses that we almost never wear and ski jackets with at least 600 old lift tags tied to the zippers. And we should love places like Vail and Aspen where everybody is blond and cool and they think our national bird is the Private Jet—and you can get a cup of coffee for twelve bucks.

We know what we're supposed to do. There is just one problem. We can't ski. And if we can't comply with our state's most rudimentary stipulation, then why even worry about the other stuff. Now we don't want you to misunderstand. We have tried! But, alas, we're awful. The first time we ventured out, people told us it would be fun. Fun? We quickly realized that this sport combines two of our least favorite things— pain and cold. The spills we took made that "agony of defeat" sequence from the *Wide World of Sports* look like a mild boo-boo. After several limb-twisting spills, we considered strapping our skis to our behinds, where they would do the most good.

The only thing worse than all the falling is skiing so slowly and carefully that we get passed by hundreds of tiny children wearing only ski goggles and Huggies. We loathe the way these tots stare at us as they whiz by—as if we were clumsy ectomorphic freaks.

Our Youth Pastor, Brant, once told us that skiing is as easy as falling down a mountain. The liar. We can fall down a mountain, no problem. Skiing down one is another story. "I'll go slowly and teach you," he promised us on one trip. "I'm a good teacher."

Here's what we have to say about Brant's lesson: If your idea of teaching skiing is taking two uncoordinated neophytes (say, us, for example) and dropping them off on one of those extreme cliffs (like the ones in the Mountain Dew commercials) and yelling, "Go for it, brothers! Keep your tips up! I'm prayin' for ya, dudes!"—if that's your approach, we don't need your help. Let's face it. We'll never be skiers. We maintain that if God had wanted people to ski, He'd have given them long, pointy fiberglass feet.

And we're willing to live with the shame—people wagging their heads sadly from side to side and saying, "You're from Colorado and you don't ski?"

We know; it's like being from Boston and not eating beans, or from Seattle and not playing in a grunge-rock band, or from North Dakota and not . . . well, not doing whatever they do up there.

Frankly though, we do worry that one day we'll learn that our Colorado citizenship has been revoked.

Some band of ski enforcers with multiple knee surgery scars and white rings around their eyes will tie us up with colorful bandannas and cart us over the Wyoming border.

Still we hope for the best. We believe that the world is big enough for all of us. Besides, we figure that the true ski buffs will appreciate that there will be a few less guys getting in the way, clogging the slopes, and bleeding all over the nice clean snow. We're doing skiers everywhere a favor by staying home.

We maintain that if God had wanted people to ski, He'd have given them long, pointy fiberglass feet.

Now if only we could convince others to take our enlightened approach—persuade bad drivers to stay off the roads, convince shoppers with twenty-eight food items to avoid the "express line," encourage bad singers not to sing church solos. . . . Nah, it will never happen. At least not in Colorado.

Most people knew not to bother Dad on
Sunday afternoons. But not the Haggerty sisters,
Babs and Editha, ages eighty-eight and
eighty-nine and a half.

He's Closer Than
You Think

It's a Hafer family tradition. During the NFL season, we all race from church to Dad's house to watch the Denver Broncos on TV. This tradition is especially meaningful for Dad. He's been following the Broncos since their infancy, and he prays for their success as fervently as he prays for warm water in the baptistery.

On Bronco Sundays, Dad is barely in the front door before he starts shedding whatever hideous polyester suit he wore to the service. He strips to his T-shirt and jockey shorts, settles into his overstuffed recliner, and for the next three hours fixes his eyes on the twenty-four-inch high-resolution color TV.

Most people in the church know not to bother Dad on Sunday afternoons. But not everyone. The Haggerty sisters, Babs and Editha Haggerty, ages eighty-eight and eighty-nine and a half, love to pop in for Sunday afternoon visits. During the off-season, Dad welcomes their invasions, especially since they usually bring pie. But during a Bronco game? Forget it.

"Ah, criminy-crock!" he wails when he sees their melon-pink Renault Le Car pull into the driveway. "Cherie, those dear sweet old ladies are here again. Please be a pal and get rid of 'em. Quick. Kickoff is in five minutes."

For five straight seasons, Mom was able to deflect the Haggertys' Bronco Sunday offensives. She'd greet them at the door, smile and say, "Good to see you, Babs and Editha! But we're kinda tied up right now."

"Oh, I see," Babs would say. "Doing something religious?"

"Yes," Mom would reply, without stretching the truth one micron.

That was usually enough to deter the Haggertys. They'd slip Mom a pie and amble back to their Le Car.

But one Sunday last season during a game with serious playoff ramifications, they arrived in a particularly persistent mood.

"We simply must see Pastor Dale," Babs insisted. (Yes, our Dad's name is Del, but in twenty years we haven't been able to convince the sisters of that fact.) "Today's sermon about the widow's might truly impressed us! It's about time somebody gave widows credit for being mighty! You know Editha here can lift a fifty-pound sack of manure right over her head!"

Mom carefully positioned herself across the door's threshold like a night-club bouncer. But on this day, Babs and Editha would not be denied. They moved toward Mom slowly, but with determination, like two hyenas approaching a wounded zebra.

Mom shot a desperate glance at Dad, who was relaxing in his chair in his undergarments, just out of the Haggertys' line of sight. "I can't stop them!" she mouthed to Dad.

At that moment, using a huckleberry pie as battering ram, the Haggertys pushed their way past Mom.

Quick as a rattlesnake strike, Dad shot into our living room coat closet, barely depriving the sisters of their frequent request to "see more of our pastor."

Once inside, Babs and Editha quickly made themselves comfortable. Babs took Dad's chair. Editha went to the kitchen to cut the pie. "Oh, my," Babs said. "I can't believe you're watching football. That's such a violent sport. You know, I think *Heidi* is on today. Such an edifying story. Couldn't we watch that instead?"

After consuming two pieces of pie each, the Haggertys began to wonder about Dad. "Cherie, where is Dale?" Editha asked. "We'd so like to see him. I have just a couple of questions to ask about the mission program."

Quick as a rattlesnake strike, Dad shot into our living room coat closet, barely depriving the sisters of their frequent request to "see more of our pastor."

"Uh," Mom began, "he's . . . around. He's maybe even closer than you think. However, I don't want to keep you here waiting for him to show up. If you don't mind me saying so, you both look a bit weary. I can have him call you when he gets in."

"Hey, don't worry about us," Babs said. "We're feeling just fine, and we really don't have a single thing to do today, do we Editha?" Then turning to the TV, she exclaimed, "My-my! Doesn't that young fella look lovely in his lederhosen! And wait till you hear him yodel!"

Now all of us Hafers love the Broncos just as much as Dad does. But the sting of missing the game was lessened by the thought of Dad scrunched in the six-by-six-foot coat closest. With all of the clothes, tennis rackets, and shoes, there was little space for a burly preacher. That closet is also where Mom keeps her accordion. (She can play two songs: "Pop, Goes the Weasel" and "How Great Thou Art.") We could almost feel the rage and frustration radiating from the closet.

Our thoughts of Dad were shattered by Babs' voice: "Cherie, these are quite interesting after-dinner mints. Are they homemade or store-bought?"

Mom looked with puzzlement at the small plate Babs was holding. The Hafers are not an after-dinner-mint kind of family. After dinner we crave something bigger and sweeter than a puny mint. A Ding-Dong or Ho-Ho for example.

Mom studied the plate and recoiled in horror at what she saw. It was loaded with Dad's toenails. Part of Dad's Bronco tradition, you see, is attending to various personal grooming tasks during commercials. Mom had repeatedly begged him to refrain from clipping his toenails or nose hairs or flossing his teeth in the living room, but to no avail.

Mom didn't want to tell near-sighted Babs the truth about the little crescent-shaped "mints" on the plate before her. But it was only a matter of time before Babs braved eating one. So Mom did the only thing she could do. She approached Babs and sneezed with all her might, blowing the toenails safely to the floor.

"I'm so sorry, Babs," Mom said. "My allergies are really acting up today."

Then a sly grin crept across Mom's face. We knew what that meant. She was angry that Dad hadn't honored her request about personal grooming decorum. Now it was pay-back time.

"Well, ladies," Mom said, easing onto the couch, "tell me about your lives. Babs, I want to hear all about your gardening—and your goiter. And, Editha, I must hear every detail about your twelve adult children, and their extended families."

"Oh, that could take a while," Editha said with a laugh.

"That's okay. I want you both to stay for dinner. I'll slow-cook a roast. And I do mean sssslow."

Four hours later, our cuckoo clock chirped that it was six o'clock.

"Oh, goodness me!" Babs exclaimed. "Can it be that late already? We should have been in bed fifteen minutes ago!"

So, full of huckleberry pie and roast, the sisters tottered out the door.

As soon as he heard the front door close, Dad, now with the posture of Quasimodo, stormed from the closet and searched desperately for the remote. He quickly clicked back to KOA, the official station of the Denver Broncos.

". . . my what a game!" the announcer gushed. "The Broncos win on a fifty-eight-yard field goal with just one second left in overtime! I've never seen anything like that. Have you, Phil?"

"Indeed I have not, Bruiser. In fact next to the birth of my twins, this is the single greatest spectacle I have ever witnessed. I feel blessed to have seen it. I shall never forget it as long as I live!"

* * * * * * * * * *

We'd like to tell you that Dad learned his lesson that day, but that would be only partially true. He doesn't clip, trim, or floss in the living room anymore. He still does, however, enjoy the Broncos while in a less-than-fully attired state. "A guy's gotta be comfortable when he watches football," he maintains.

Three other implications sprang from that day. First, Dad doesn't enjoy his favorite chair as much anymore. He says it just doesn't sit right. Second, none of us are allowed to name our children Babs or Editha— or Heidi. And finally, Dad is now prepared for the Haggertys. He has banished Mom's accordion from the front closet to the garage. In its place rests a twelve-inch portable color TV he bought at a garage sale for thirty-eight bucks, just in case.

Mrs. Klefcorn had skin, and a personality, like beef jerky. She stood in front of our Sunday school class, her hairdo the same height and density as the hats worn by those British guards at Buckingham Palace.

Todd Wields the Sword:
His Own Story

I'll never forget how the competitive tension hung in the air like smoke. The anxiety gnawed at my stomach, and the steely determination of my foes flashed in their eyes.

I had been practicing all week, working on every facet of my performance. I knew once the weekend came I had to be ready. I'd be up against fierce competitors—many crazed by steroids—firm in their resolve not only to defeat me, but to humiliate me as well.

Yes, those third-grade Sunday school sword drills were rough. What? You thought I was talking about my days as a high school football player? Get real. No coach was ever as harsh as Mrs. Klefcorn, and no gridiron battle was as fierce as those played out in the cold basement of Broomfield Baptist Church.

I can still envision Mrs. Klefcorn with skin—and a personality—like beef jerky, standing in front of our class. Her hairdo was the same height and density as the hats worn by the guards at Buckingham Palace, and in one hand she held a yardstick which she'd snap loudly on the craft table if we got too noisy. In the other hand, she held a big, black, intimidating King James Bible. For years the rumor had circulated that King James himself had given that Bible to Mrs. Klefcorn, but it was never confirmed.

Mrs. K would begin each class the same way. She'd set her jaw and rotate her head like a tank turret to ensure she had everyone's attention. Then the words would leap from her mouth: "It's time to drill! Swords in the air!"

Almost in unison, we would raise our Bibles high overhead. Then we would all lean forward, waiting for Mrs. K to announce the first reference. I know that some of you probably participated in sword drills in which you had to find only a particular book of the Bible. I mean no disrespect, but such drills are for wimps. With Mrs. K, you had to find chapter and verse then spring to your feet and read it aloud.

On one particular Sunday, I arrived in class riding a two-week winning streak. But I was nervous. Timmy Waller was back from vacation in the Ozarks, looking tanned and ready. I knew his dad, a deacon, had probably held family devotions every day of their vacation. During his two-week absence, he'd probably heard most of the Bible read to him. The cheater.

Then out of the corner of my eye, I saw Judy Bittle, holding her dusty-rose petite KJV in her white gloved hands. Another cheater. Those so-called fashion gloves virtually eliminated the slippage associated with sweaty palms. Judy had used this trick before, and I'd thought of filing a grievance with the Sunday school board. But Sparky Klein told me that while gloves were helpful in the gripping department, they could also reduce digital dexterity by up to 9 percent. So I had decided to keep my mouth shut.

My thoughts were shattered by Mrs. K's foghorn voice: "Matthew 6:19!" In a nanosecond, my Bible was open, my fingers flash-flipping through the pages. Habakkuk—dunder! Classic mistake. I hadn't opened far enough. Feeling the heat, I plunged forward. Epistles to the Romans—arrrgh! Too far! I backtracked. Ah-hah! Matthew at last! Now if I could just get to chapter six in time. Timmy and I shot to our feet in perfect unison. But he had made a fatal strategic error. While rising he had forgotten to keep his finger on the verse! *Maybe next time, loser!*

As he scanned the page in a panic, I was already reading, "Lay not up for yourselves treasures upon earth, where moth and rust doth corrupt, and where thieves break through and steal."

Mrs. K smiled at me. Or at least I think it was a smile. It could have been gas. "Very well done, Todd," she said. "Timmy was close, but maybe he's missed just a wee bit too much Sunday school this month. Now, Todd, you may come up to the Bible Bounty Treasure Chest and claim your prize."

Lay not up for yourselves treasures upon earth, I recited in my head as I strutted to the chest. In compliance with the rules, I closed my eyes as I thrust my hand deep into the chest. Right away I felt something steel and grabbed it. Steel meant quality. Not like those cheap plastic disciples that broke the first time you played army with them. "Moth and rust, moth and rust," I hummed as I pulled out my prize and eyed it proudly. It was a bank shaped like the earth!

I lost that bank long ago, but I haven't forgotten Matthew 6:19, or my introduction to the concept of irony.

Anna Baptist: "John, your breath smells awful!
Have you been eating locusts again?"
John: "Yeah, they're not too bad. Taste a little
like chicken. Would you like to try one?"

Anna Baptist

A few years ago while Jedd and I were team-teaching a Sunday school class, the subject of the Anabaptists came up. One kid asked, "What's an Anabaptist?"

"You bonehead," another scolded. "Anna Baptist was John the Baptist's wife!"

We all enjoyed a good chuckle that day, but the episode got us thinking—did John the Baptist have a wife? If so, could her name have been Anna? We began to wonder. . . .

We imagined Anna Baptist trudging into the wilderness to visit her husband and begging him to come home:

"Johnny, how long are you going to stay out here? Can't you come home at least for the weekend? My parents have invited us for dinner."

John, of course, would have been happy to see his wife. But not enough to change his plans:

"Oh, hi there, Anna. It's good to see you, but I can't come home just yet. I've got way too much work to do. Gotta get people to repent. Gotta deal with the People for the Ethical Treatment of Animals who are protesting my camel hair outfit. Gotta confront the various denominational groups that are wooing me. Some want me to become John the Episcopalian. Others think John the Presbyterian would be more effective. I've pretty much ruled out John the Congregationalist."

"Oh, Johnny!"

"Don't cry, Anna. I'll be home soon. Come on now, let's have a hug."

"I can't, Johnny. That camel's hair jacket gives me a rash. By the way, lose the belt. It really doesn't go with your outfit."

"Okay ... wait! Your breath smells awful! Have you been eating locusts again?"

"Oh. Well then, how about a little kiss at least?"

"Okay . . . wait! Your breath smells awful! Have you been eating locusts again?"

"Well, yeah. They're not too bad. Taste a bit like chicken. Would you like to try one?"

"I'll pass. Good-bye, John."

"Wait, don't leave like that. No hugs, no kisses? Won't you at least join me for a quick swim?"

"Well . . . okay. But no dunking!"

Pew-trefaction

Throughout our church-going lives, there have been any number of Christianese terms that have disturbed and baffled us. One of those terms is "pew." As a rule, the Hafer brothers have tried hard to avoid anything remotely connected with the concept of pew. We don't want to talk about pew, especially during dinner. We don't want to look at pew, and we certainly don't want to smell pew. But every Sunday we go to church and sit in a pew.

Why are church seating facilities called pews anyway? We have asked every clergical person we know, and still we have not been given a reasonable explanation. Are pews named for their inventor? Perhaps it was someone by the name of Leopold Pew who first envisioned long, hard, uncomfortable benches in churches across this great land. When you think about it, it's a clever way to keep parishioners awake during the service. It's more practical and humane than having ushers creep through the congregation, thumping dozers behind the ears or poking them in the ribs.

Leopold Pew was probably a pastor—an egotistical pastor. We think a guy named Fritz Goiter invented the hot dog, but he didn't insist on calling his creation the hot goiter or even just plain goiters. He foresaw the awkwardness of a street vendor asking a patron, "Would you like mustard and onions on your goiter, ma'am?"

Not so with Leopold. He had to force the issue and get his name in lights, or at least in the church bulletin periodically. He had to forever pollute the air of those pre-service conversations. When we should be discussing supralapsarianism, back-masking on Hanson albums, and other important topics, we are instead preoccupied with pews.

Perhaps it was someone by the name of Leopold Pew who first envisioned long, hard, uncomfortable benches in churches across this great land.

"Say, the front two pews are roped off this morning. We must be having some special guests. Maybe the Brady Bunch have all become Christians and moved here!"

"What this church needs is more pew space. We need new pews."

"Boy, there's a lot of varnish on the pews this week; I can hardly slide at all."

"You said it. I prefer a light coat of varnish, well-buffed, so you can slide like Ricky Henderson."

In some churches, you can even remember loved ones by putting an engraved plaque on a pew. Now there's a strange way to immortalize someone. Name a pew after 'em. We're not sure this is an appropriate remembrance unless the deceased was a department store Santa and accustomed to having people sit on him all the time.

Unfortunately, the term "pew" is probably here to stay. And as we think about it, "blessed bleachers," "sanctified slabs o'pine," and "beatific benches" don't sound that great either.

But it still cracks us up to hear people saying "pew" so much in church. You'd think the term would be reserved for the nursery.

A few years ago when Todd was single, an attractive girl approached him in church.

"Is this pew saved?" she asked.

Todd smiled warmly. "It isn't, but I am!" he sputtered. *Totally* impressed, she turned without a word and sat in someone else's pew.

A Foyer by Any Other Name . . .

Another annoying problem we've encountered is that no one knows what to call that certain place in the church where one will find such items as the *Our Daily Bread,* the attendance board that hasn't been updated in eight months, and the "Community Cupboard" donation box with three cans of sweet peas and a gallon jar of sauerkraut. Some of the choices are:

The "narthex."

The "vestibule."

The "foyer."

The "lobby."

. . . or, if you're really spiritual—the "fellowship area."

It's amazing how strongly some people feel about this issue. You can spark some hot debate by bringing it up at your next "Get-Up-Early-for-Heaven's-Sake Prayer Breakfast" or "Ladle-on-the-Love Couples Retreat and Wallyball Tournament."

To help ignite your discussion, here is our perspective on the issue.

"Lobby" is out. It's too theater oriented. Plus, it has unsavory political connotations.

"Foyer" rhymes with lawyer. Need we say more?

"Vestibule" sounds too medical: "I'm sorry to tell you this, Mr. Noggin, but we've found a vestibule on your spleen."

So that leaves us with "fellowship area" and "narthex." This is a tough call, but we're going to have to go with the latter. "Fellowship area" is okay, but it's just so religiously correct.

> Foyer" rhymes with lawyer. Need we say more?

"Narthex" is crisper, more in step with the future. Plus, it might attract more men to church, because it sounds like the name of a sports arena. (Booming Voice): "Sunday at the Narthex, feel the thunder of the Reverend Mammoth Monster Mike Maddox as he exegetes the entire book of Habakkuk! Experience the raw power of Melchizedek Barnes and the Holy Smokin' Choir! They're hotter than a nitro-burning funny car! Admission is free (Just please bring a can of sweet peas). That's S-S-S-S-S-Sunday at the Narthex! Be there! The pews are already shaking! Feel the POWER!!!"

Remembering Grandpa Jim

(A tribute originally presented by
Todd at Grandpa's funeral)

My grandpa Jim died in the same hospital where I was born. In the thirty-plus years between those two events, he blessed me with "a thousand purty songs" (a few of which I don't think he learned as a member of his church choir), ten thousand jokes (which I hope he didn't hear at church), and at least a million of my fondest memories.

There is so much I'll always remember about Grandpa Jim: He'd drive for hours—even days—to visit his children and grandchildren; he'd let my brothers and me take turns sitting in his "rumble seat" while he popped popcorn for us; the way he would let us run around in his auto repair shop; the sight of him crawling out from under some clunker to buy us a pop from his cooler; and the taste of his homemade ice cream. (I'm not sure exactly how the ancient ice cream maker worked. Somehow rock salt and snow were involved. But it made the best ice cream I've ever tasted.)

Grandpa could figure out how to fix anything. He could take apart any appliance, state the diagnosis ("its pizzle is sprung"), then put it back together, running more smoothly than when it was new.

I especially remember the day he and I rotated the tires on my Toyota, and how at age eighty he jumped up and down on the lug wrench to loosen a stubborn nut and tossed the tires around like they were made of Styrofoam. Seven years before, he had been diagnosed with cancer and sent home to die. But the doctors underestimated the power of prayer.

My son T.J. used to toddle around, following Grandpa Jim wherever he went. He loved to watch the old master move from room to room, fixing everything in sight. He asked Grandpa a million questions, telling him, "When I grow up, I want to use real tools like you have—not toy ones!"

Grandpa seemed to enjoy the company. I can still hear his rumbling baritone voice singing T.J. some of those "thousand purty songs."

He'd start off with a few hymns, like "When the Roll Is Called Up Yonder" and "Bringing in the Sheaves" then segue into some numbers he must have learned in the Navy, such as "Don't Dance on My Table, Mabel."

Grandpa had a temper when it came to foreign cars, politicians, and those "dad-gummed Denver Broncos," but he never said a harsh word to his family.

One more thing, Grandpa loved Jesus, zealously. He was a fixture in his church choir, and he repaired many a parishioner's car, often getting nothing more than a "God bless you" as payment. One Sunday after his pastor encouraged the congregation to evangelize their neighborhoods, Grandpa went out knocking on doors in an area of south Denver that even Hulk Hogan would have avoided. Despite rejection after rejection, Jim kept going. He came back more angry than discouraged. "Nobody in this whole neighborhood even wants to hear about Jesus," he fumed. "I got so mad I felt like telling the whole lot of them to go jump off a bridge!" That was Grandpa Jim.

I miss all those songs, all those jokes—okay, some of the jokes, his hearty "Helloooo!" when I walk into my Grandma's tiny, white house. And I miss shaking those strong hands with the permanent grease under the fingernails.

But I'm glad Grandpa's pain is gone and that he's where he wanted to be. Heaven will never be the same.

Neither will earth.

You see, there are so many things still broken here—like hearts for one thing. And now there's one less person to help fix them.

As I think about it, Grandpa Jim's best tools weren't the socket set or the spark-plug wrench. They were his indestructible sense of humor and his childlike faith. I'll never be the mechanic Grandpa Jim was. I couldn't even name half the tools he used expertly, much less repair anything with them.

But those other tools, the spiritual ones. Those I understand thanks to Grandpa Jim. I hope I can use them as well as he did.

Potlucks: Not Always Good Fortune

The "potluck" dinner is a tradition as old as the Jell-O mold itself. It has been a revered Christian tradition since churches moved from tents into buildings with electric ovens and indoor plumbing, and trust us, it will continue to be an important part of church life as long as leftovers lie brooding in parishioners' freezers.

In fact to this day, our Mom has a Deepfreeze full of stuff that's been frozen longer than Walt Disney. Every spring we urge her to throw out her many frost-covered Ziplock bags, but her reply is always the same: "I can't throw this stuff out. I'm saving it for the next potluck!"

We can't be sure of the exact origin of the potluck concept, but we did hear from a reliable source that it was the brainchild of a pastor who resided somewhere in the Midwest. It seems that one Friday night, he was struck by an inspiration: "Hey, my family members are the only ones who get to taste the worst food in our house! What fun is that? What if the whole church got together once a month and sampled the most horrific cuisine, the most cryogenically entombed leftovers from every household? It's crazy, perhaps even a little dangerous, but I think it could promote bonding within the congregation and provide a stronger sense of community—if it doesn't kill us first."

This gustatory epiphany quickly swept through churches nationwide. And it came to pass that folks soon began arriving at church, toting paper plates, twelve-pound tuna casseroles, enough Swedish meatballs to feed all of Sweden, and Jell-O sufficient to drown a woolly mammoth.

> Large adults wedged themselves into metal folding chairs and spilled instant pink lemonade on themselves.

Church goers were encouraged to "come to the fellowship area and enjoy the food, fun, and fellowship!" Long lines formed, children stuck their fingers into black olives and staged boxing matches. (These bouts, along with cock fights, are now illegal in most states.) Large adults wedged themselves into metal folding chairs and spilled instant pink lemonade on themselves. People laughed heartily, then asked suspiciously, "Who made the corn pone?" A tradition was born.

But just because the potluck is a sacred tradition doesn't mean it can't be improved or enjoyed more thoroughly by the savvy potluck goer. Here are a few tips to keep your potlucks from going to pot:

1. Add variety by sending your spouse or significant other out for pizza or chicken. Many people will thank you for this. We don't encourage you to put the take-out food in a casserole dish and try to pass it off as home cookin', but you probably won't invoke divine judgment if you fudge just a bit. Think of it as bringing a blessing in disguise:

"Hey, Marv, this chicken is down-home delicious. You fry it yourself?"

"Why no, an old army buddy of mine made it. Fella named Sanders. He's a colonel."

2. The brownies may look good, but they were actually prepared by a parishioner's eight-year-old daughter (probable name: Naomi) and taste exactly like small squares of sod.

3. You can never go wrong with macaroni 'n cheese if you throw in tiny squares of meat for protein's sake. One warning here though, it has to be the right meat. For example:

> Ham = good
> Hamburger = OK
> Spam = pushing it
> Recently thawed red snapper = not good
> Panda meat = very bad
> Anything that ends with the words "meat by-product" = induce vomiting.

4. When selecting a little plate with a slice of cake on it, choose a corner piece. You get more frosting that way, and even an inept cook can't mess up frosting.

5. Eat the Jell-O early or it will liquefy, and you'll be sucking shredded carrots and banana chips through your teeth.

6. Never argue with Mrs. Swensen about her famous fifteen-bean salad. Case in point:

"Mrs. Swensen, there aren't fifteen kinds of beans in the whole world! What kind of scam are you trying to pull?"

"Yes, there are! Navy, kidney, lima, pinto, Mexican jumping . . . uh, jelly?"

7. Never eat Mrs. Swensen's famous fifteen-bean salad.

8. Clearly label all dishes. Once we mistook a potpourri centerpiece for trail mix. It tasted terrible, but our breath did carry a lovely elderberry pine scent for the next week.

9. Make sure you pay attention to which cup you drink from. There's nothing worse than mistakenly grabbing some kid's cup and drinking eight partially chewed Cheerios and a Star Wars action figure in a thick saliva base.

10. Most important of all: Never, ever, ever, bring devil's food cake, not even as a joke.

How to Be a Meat Loafer

You've just read the chapter about potluck dinners, and now you're psyched to create something memorable for your next big church chow-fest. We want to help you. We really do. So in a splendiferous show of good faith, we have decided to share a treasured family recipe that we stole from our friend Robin. It's for the yummy and filling "Genuine Ten-Pound Double-Wide Meat Loaf."

We know that some of you are frightened by the mere thought of meat loaf. We understand. Let's face it, meat balls are a non-threatening food item, as are the larger but flatter meat patties. But a whole loaf of meat is daunting to prepare as well as to consume.

We feel that we should all be grateful that no one has invented the meat pile yet or the meat mountain, which is cooked for several days over a bonfire on the outskirts of town. When it's done, the town folk converge on it armed only with forks and a hearty appetite.

Now that we have some perspective on the matter, on to our once-secret, still-coveted recipe.

Genuine Ten-Pound Double-Wide Meat Loaf

First, buy a generous quantity of ground beef. Purists disagree on what percentage of fat the meat should contain. Some say our ancestors would use only the greasiest meats available at the local supermarket. However, we contend that the fat percentage is irrelevant. You see, a true double-wide meat loaf is by definition cooked to death. In its most perfect form, it should have the flavor and density of a partially inflated NFL football. Therefore, we encourage you to use lean beef. It dries out quicker, doesn't shrink too much, and emerges from the oven with a refined but unpretentious ebony hue.

We encourage you to use lean beef. It dries out quicker, doesn't shrink too much, and emerges from the oven with a refined but unpretentious ebony hue.

In any case, once you've chosen your meat, put it in a huge, plastic bowl (the one your kids used as a wading pool when they were younger) and add any or all of the following: potato chips, corn flakes, ketchup, extra spicy Slim Jims, grits, Tobasco, lard, and Jolt cola.

Next, toss in some Cheez-Whiz, Cheetos, Cheezy Puffs, or Cheez-Its—any item that has a variation of the word "cheese" in its name but contains no actual dairy products will do nicely. At this point, you're on a roll, so pile on some freezer-burned veggies, canned okra, and white bread. Under no circumstances should you include any of the following items: Grey Poupon mustard, brie, Shitaake mushrooms, cocktail sauce, scallions, shallots, or anything with an expiration date before the year 2008. To include such items would make a mockery of our proud heritage.

Now, wrestle with this mess until you've taught it who's raw meat and who's the next step up the food chain. Call your significant other to help you heft the loaf into the oven. Bake at your oven's highest temperature for the duration of one *Dukes of Hazzard* rerun.

The meat loaf is done when the smoke in your kitchen wafts through your screen door and sets off the smoke alarm in your neighbor's home.

The Funeral of Mr. Steak

How did you spend your Saturdays when you were a kid—watching cartoons, playing in the park, going to the movies? If any of these options sound familiar, you're probably not a pastor's kid. If you were, you'd have answered, "Going to weddings and funerals that our dad was officiating."

Yes, a P.K. sees more people married and buried than almost anyone. Almost every Saturday we had to don our dorky seventies church clothes and attend solemn ceremonies for people we'd never met. We hated it, and it scarred us, but we're not bitter.

In fact now that we're more mature, we sometimes choose to accompany Dad as he officiates at these events. Probably because we are still intrigued by the question: How does one officiate a funeral? Is it similar to how one would officiate a football game? What kind of penalties could you call at a funeral? Intentional grounding? Unnecessary stiffness? Kicking the bucket?

Another reason that we like to attend is that it's intriguing to observe the behavior and attitudes of people encountering two of life's major milestones. Oh yeah, and the food is usually quite good—especially when your refrigerator is empty except for 1,000 packets of Taco Bell mild sauce.

We've seen amazing weddings, such as the one in which the bride marched down the aisle with a strip of toilet paper stuck to her heel, dragging ceremoniously behind her.

At another wedding, the uncle charged with videotaping the event strategically placed his camera directly below a high-powered ceiling fan, like those used to create tornadoes in the movie *Twister*. He got great video, but the audio portion sounded like it was recorded in one of those radio traffic helicopters. *"Skkkkkkkkk crackle crackle skkkkk* Both side aisles are *skkkkk* clear and running smoothly, *crackle, ping, crackle* but we're seeing some slowing on the main *thththththththth* aisle, as people stop to gawk at the bride's father, *ssskkkkkkkkk* whose toupee seems to be askew *crackle crackle ping skkkkkkk thththththth."*

The uncle tried to get Dad and the bride and groom to redo the vows and dub them into the video. The result was like one of those old Godzilla movies, without the total destruction of Tokyo:

Dad: (lips not moving) Do you, Bernice, take Clyde (lips still not moving) to be your (now lips move a lot) husband?

Bernice: (lips moving) . . .

Godzilla: "Raaaaarrrrrgh!"

Our most memorable ceremony, however, was the funeral of a man named Daniel Steak. It was a lovely service, almost without incident—until near the end. That is when, for some reason, Dad blanked on the name of the deceased. He said, ". . . and so we commend now, the soul of the departed . . . the departed . . ."

At this point, the second half of the man's name popped into his head. So he said, "We commend to you the soul of Mr. Steak." Now that would have worked out just fine, except that Mr. Steak is a popular restaurant in Colorado. Ironically, there was one down the street from the church.

We were so overcome with laughter that we teetered on the brink of embarrassing our dad and ourselves, along with being banned from the buffet. We had to regain our composure. We looked at each other knowingly, realizing that our only hope was to concentrate our thoughts on something completely not funny. So we thought of Pauly Shore. And we were okay for a while, until Dad's next sentence, "He was a rare individual, a warm and tender man, taken away in the prime of his life."

> "He was a rare individual, a warm and tender man, taken away in the prime of his life."

At this point, we did what any mature Christian young men would do. We shook with laughter, tears streaming down our faces, and instituted "the cover," a cherished technique passed down through the ages by clergy of all denominations. Burying our faces in our hands, we pretended to be completely overcome with emotion. We were just regaining our composure when Mr. Steak's brother, a beefy man named Chuck got up to say a few words. At this point, Dad bowed his head and joined us in this ancient custom.

That day we were all fortunate that laughter and sobbing are so closely related. Everyone approached Dad after the funeral to say what a beautiful ceremony it was. We joined in the congratulations. "Yeah, Dad," we said. "Well done!"

The P.K. Top Ten List

As pastor's kids, we have been asked many questions, such as, "Could you please refrain from dating my daughter?" and "For the love of Pete, could you please, please refrain from dating my daughter?!?"

However, the most frequent question posed to us is, "What are the pros and cons of growing up as P.K.'s? Tell us about the good, the bad, the ugly." Here now, in the ever-popular top ten format, is our answer:

The Ten Best Things about Growing Up As Preacher's Kids

1. Getting to eat leftovers from potluck dinners.
2. Hanging out with other dysfunctional P.K.'s at summer church camps, and realizing we weren't as messed up as we thought.
3. Having command of King James English will come in handy if we ever decide to become Shakespearean actors.

4. Always being assured of starting point guard and center positions on church basketball team.

5. Making extra money by telling church newcomers that the bulletins were "programs" and charging twenty-five cents apiece.

6. Sneaking into the church late at night, cranking up the sound system, and pretending to be rock stars.

7. Sneaking into church late at night and doing cannonball dives into the baptistery. (We don't recommend this for Presbyterians.)

8. Building massive muscles by bench-pressing Dad's set of exhaustive biblical commentaries.

9. Setting the electric organ to "rock beat" on Saturday night, freaking out the organist on Sunday morning.

10. After seeing Dad's tireless and ingenious efforts to recruit Sunday school teachers, we're well equipped for successful careers in telemarketing.

The Ten Worst Things about Growing Up As Preacher's Kids

1. Eating leftovers from potluck dinners. (Yeah, this was on the other list, too. It all depends.)

2. Getting in trouble for trying to start "The Wave" during lulls in Dad's sermons.

3. Having every stupid thing we ever said and did used as a sermon illustration.

4. Always being called on to answer the tough questions in Sunday school: (i.e., "Todd, how would you solve the epistemological conundrum posed by Solomon in Ecclesiastes 1?")

5. No chance of our family ever sleeping in so we could watch the first game of the NFL double-header on Sunday.

6. Never getting a date with the choir director's daughters, even with snappy pick-up lines like, "Hey, baby, what's your spiritual gift?"

7. Trying to hit the high notes on "Bringing in the Sheaves" while going through puberty.

8. Getting in trouble for telling Sunday school peers that Joan of Arc was Noah's wife.

9. Getting in more trouble for putting a picture of Moses on the church rest room with the caption "Let my people go!"

10. Every Halloween Dad would come in and demand we tithe him 10 percent of our candy!

Our favorite member of the music militia,
Mrs. Smithstein, will waddle to the stage,
toting a tuba the size of a Sherman tank.
As she plays, her face grows redder and redder.
The congregation finds it hard not to
burst out laughing. Mrs. Smithstein
finds it hard not to burst, period.

Special Music:
What to Do When It's Not So Special

Music has never been a strong point at Broomfield Baptist Church. Most of our congregation thinks a cantata is an entree at Taco Bell. Thus, one of the greatest tests of our self-control during worship services is the "special music." (AKA the "ministry in music," the "witness in song," or "a husband and wife with a guitar and too much free time.")

At most churches, a talented individual from the congregation will select an appropriate Amy Grant or Steven Curtis Chapman back-up tape, add a few tasteful dance moves, and deliver a pleasant sounding, spiritually uplifting performance.

At BBC a farmer named Clem will sing "Do Lord," accompanying himself with the musical spoons. Or our favorite member of the music militia, Mrs. Smithstein, will waddle to the stage, toting a tuba the size of a Sherman tank. Mrs. Smithstein typically graces us with two or twelve old-time gospel favorites. Frightened children scatter as Mrs. S's face grows redder and redder. Adults find it hard not to burst out laughing; Mrs. S finds it hard not to burst—period.

When Mrs. S and her tuba are finished assaulting some perfectly innocent songs, our dad will come to her side and say something like, "Thank you, Mrs. Smithstein. Those . . . uh, songs were uniquely and sincerely rendered." That's because he can't say, "Your tuba playing sounds like a herd of flatulent wildebeests."

Dad's responses to Mrs. Smithstein are perfect—subtly honest and inoffensive. This is important because it would be wrong to be too blunt. That would hurt Mrs. Smithstein. And she has a right hook that can take down a bison.

How many people in the whole world can yodel "Bringing in the Sheaves" while accompanying themselves on the accordion?

So if you ever find yourself in the awkward position of trying to compliment someone in your church after he or she has butchered your favorite song, follow Reverend Hafer's lead. For example:

"I gotta tell you, Wendell, when Martin Luther wrote 'A Mighty Fortress' hundreds of years ago, I bet he never envisioned that one day you'd play his masterpiece on a homemade wax-paper-and-comb kazoo!"

Or, "Wow, Mrs. Gackout! How many people in the whole world can yodel 'Bringing in the Sheaves' while accompanying themselves on the accordion? Dressing as Heidi was a nice touch, as well."

Hafers aren't known for their extraordinary tact and diplomacy, but we have learned not to discourage people from sharing their gifts. So give this technique a try. It's important to make your local minstrels feel special—because they are—even when their music isn't.

During the invitation one Sunday, King,
our English Shepherd/Border Collie/Sheltie/
Pomeranian, came forward, eyes repentant,
tongue lolling from his mouth.

The Day King Got Saved

It was a sweltering summer Sunday back in 1976. Inside Broomfield Baptist Church, it was like a sauna—without the sweaty guys in towels. The church doors were open so that some of the hot, fresh air outside could enter the sanctuary to mingle with the hot, stale air inside.

Parishioners fanned themselves with their bulletins, and we Hafer brothers fidgeted on the front pew in an effort to keep our woolen pants from being heat-fused to the wood. It was a good day for Dad to preach about hell, which he was doing. But he really didn't have to say much. The sanctuary served as a living illustration: the oven-like heat; the stench of sweat mixed with polyester and bad perfume; the weeping and wailing (from small children and the missionaries visiting from Alaska); the gnashing of teeth. (Never mind that. It was just Mrs. McCormack's dentures, and she always gnashed them because they didn't fit.) You get the point. The overall effect was quite compelling.

And so it came to pass that Dad, beads of sweat gleaming on his forehead, decided to go for the Big "I" (invitation). ". . . so if there is anyone here today who has not made a commitment," Dad intoned, "I invite you to come forward now. Remember, hell is even hotter than Broomfield in July, and property taxes are higher there as well."

We're sure that if there were any unsaved people (or "spiritually-challenged" for you P.C.'ers), they would have come forward. But this was Broomfield Baptist Church, where the average attendee was saved in utero and baptized by the age of five. Thus, the seconds crawled by; the sanctuary grew hotter; women's make-up began to melt.

From our reserved seats on the front pew, we heard heavy panting. I turned to Jedd and nodded, knowing we were thinking the same thing. *Probably Mrs. McCormack overheating like a bad radiator.*

"Just a few more moments," Dad gasped. "Is there anyone out there who would come forward?"

From our reserved seats on the front pew, we heard heavy panting. I turned to Jedd and nodded, knowing we were thinking the same thing. *Probably Mrs. McCormack overheating like a bad radiator.* But then the panting grew louder, closer, accompanied by a low whimper. Poor Mrs. McCormack. We turned to look at her in her misery, but we saw him instead.

It was King, our English shepherd/border collie/sheltie/Pomeranian. He was headed down the aisle; his eyes repentant, his tongue lolling from his mouth, his tail between his legs.

Perhaps King was wracked with guilt over chewing up Dad's loafers or eating our entire Christmas pot roast back in 1969. Whatever the case, King came forward that Sunday—just as he was. He didn't kneel at the front of the church, but he did sit, which is close enough don't you think?

Dad, teetering on the brink of heat exhaustion, didn't even try to explain King's presence. He merely said what every pastor says when there's nothing left to say: "Let us pray."

We could have sworn that King even bowed his head.

To this day, we're not sure if King actually got saved that Sunday. But in the weeks that followed, he was a changed dog. He quit drinking from the toilet, and he seemed to overcome his desire to sink his teeth into the paper boy's leg.

We sure hope that King did find peace in his canine conversion, because about four months after that fateful Sunday he was run over by a Hostess delivery truck, and we'd like to think we'll see him in Heaven someday. We just hope they remember to keep the church doors closed up there.

Don't Snooze in the Pews

We're embarrassed to admit it, but we occasionally struggled to stay awake in church. Sometimes the culprit would be a triple overtime, Saturday night college basketball game that forced us to stay up against our collective will.

On other occasions, a marathon Monopoly match was to blame. Our Monopoly competitions could literally last all night, unless Chadd was disqualified for cheating, or Jedd became angry and threw a hotel at Bradd, or Bradd got angry first and force-fed the Boardwalk and the little metal shoe to Jedd.

At other times, Mom's world-famous, petite pancakes were at fault. We can call her pancakes world famous because several missionaries from other continents have eaten them and talk about them to this day (e.g., "Mrs. Hafer's l'il pancakes are much tastier than the spider-monkeys back home in the jungles of Ubangi!").

The problem with Mom's choice carbohydrate cakes is that they are so tasty that we'd often eat twenty or more for Sunday morning breakfast. Then our bodies would tell us it was time to undo the top button of our dorky brown corduroy pants and stretch out on the living room floor for a two-hour nap. But we'd barely get a good nap going before Mom would yell, "Get off the floor, you little pancake-scarfing yayhoos! Comb your hair and get to Sunday school!"

Groggy and disoriented, we'd rub our eyes and stumble out the door. We usually managed to maintain the appearance of consciousness during Sunday school. The cold steel chairs forced us to sit up straight, and the eighty-seven choruses of "Do Lord" helped get our blood pumping.

But the eleven o'clock service—that was the true test of our Christian commitment. The pancake euphoria would really kick in by then. If we found it an Olympian task to pry our eyes back open after the invocation, we knew we'd never make it to the benediction, a full ninety minutes later. (Remember, this is a Baptist church we're talking about, so don't any of you Baptists get put out with us. You know we're just telling the truth.)

Back in the introduction, we said our dad was the best preacher we've ever heard. And we still maintain that. His sermons are never nap aids. But in our pancake comas, not even a pack of screaming hyenas could have kept us awake. We would fight sleep with every ounce of our will and strength. But one by one, we'd succumb to the Sunday morning sandman.

One Sunday Chadd nodded forward and rested his head on the pew in front of us just as Dad reached the fiery conclusion of his sermon about how the Pharisees were much creepier than the Saducees. "That's it," Todd said knowingly. "Chadd's out."

"Serves the cheater right," Bradd whispered. "Last night he landed on my railroad with three houses and never paid me!"

"Hey," Jedd frowned, "you can't put houses on a railroad!"

Bradd looked panicked for a moment, then regained his composure and offered his standard reply, "Shut up, loser."

Meanwhile, Chadd "passed go" and slept right through the closing hymn, the benediction, and the last-minute plea for volunteers for the rock concert carpool. When everyone headed for the Fellowship Area to eat store-bought cookies, we stayed behind to sit and stare at Chadd. He was snoring like a tractor now, and a thin strand of drool dangled from his lip, eventually adhering to the corner of the hymnal he held on his lap.

We three conscious brothers eyed him with sympathy. "He looks so peaceful, doesn't he?" Todd said quietly.

"Indeed," Bradd whispered.

We all paused for a moment and then rained noogies on Chadd's sleepy head. We may have also whooped like an Indian war party.

"Jerks!" Chadd muttered, raising his head from the pew. "I was dreaming that Candy Graham was asking me to the school dance!"

Just then Dad arrived, holding a stack of chocolate chip cookies. "What's the deal, Chadd?" he asked.

Chadd looked up at Dad and wiped the drool from his mouth. "Dad, these barbarians disturbed me in my quiet and peaceful state of meditation. I was pondering your sermon."

Dad looked at him suspiciously. "What was my sermon about, Chadd?"

"God. And Jesus. And love?"

Dad wasn't buying any of it. He sternly reprimanded Chadd for several minutes, occasionally shaking a cookie at him for emphasis. Only the fact that Dad was eager to get home and into his underwear in time for the Bronco game saved Chadd from having to scrape the gum from underneath every pew in the church.

> Only the fact that Dad was eager to get home and into his underwear in time for the Bronco game saved Chadd from having to scrape the gum from underneath every pew in the church.

Back at home, the Broncos built a huge half-time lead—a comfortable enough margin to allow Dad and Chadd to sleep comfortably through the second half.

We feel that one final note is necessary here. We must apologize to Dad for the few times that we slumbered during his sermons. But Dad, on those very rare occasions, we like to think that your profound messages still reached us on a subconscious level. Kind of like those tapes people use to learn French while they sleep. Isn't that right, Jedd?

"Jedd? Why is your head resting on the table? We have to finish this chapter! Oh, no! Come on, wake up, man!"

Well, readers, I'm not sure what to do now. I know what Chadd would say if he were here: "NOOGIE TIME!"

But lately I've been trying to follow the proverb "Noogie not, lest you be noogied." So I guess I'll just say *au revoir, mes amis.* Wait a minute that was French. Where did that come from? You don't suppose. . . .

Thank You for Calling Mega-Church

We speak at a lot of churches, and organizing these speaking forays involves hours of phone calls to churches across the nation. Sometimes we need to talk to the churches before we arrive to settle on minor details: "Okay, then. We'll speak at your Spiritual Emphasis Week beginning February 15th. Now, does that twenty-five-dollar honorarium include meal money? And as for the pickup truck we'll be sleeping in—is that parked in a garage or out on the parking lot?"

Other times, we'll need to contact the church after the fact to clarify something: "Yes, we did speak at your Youth-O-Rama last week. But, no—and we'll swear on a stack of hymnals—we did not steal the youth group's tetherball. If we were you, we'd take a hard look at the Christian mime."

Lately, as we have pursued our calling, we've observed a disturbing phone trend. More and more, we find that we're talking to machines rather than people. Don't get us wrong, we enjoy a spirited game of phone tag as much as the next roving brother act, but especially with large churches it seems to be increasingly difficult to make contact with a live human being.

When we call big churches, we often get a message like this:

"Thank you for calling Mega-Church, a subsidiary of Mondo Cathedrals, Inc. We're happy you called. Please follow these instructions carefully.

> If you'd like actual human contact, please understand that our staff is very busy growing the church.

"If you'd like to submit a prayer request, press 1, then speak clearly at the tone. Our Sancto-Vac 8000 computer will then issue an automated prayer, encoded for your security, to our Heaven-bound uplink satellite system every day for the next month. (Except on the second Tuesday of the month, when Sancto's hard-drive is being backed up.)

"If you'd like to confess some sin, press 2 and tell Sancto-Vac all about it—but please try to describe each sin in twenty-five words or less. If you have eight or fewer sins, press 22 for our express confession line. And as always, please allow four to six weeks for forgiveness.

"If you're obsessive/compulsive, press 3 over and over and over until you feel better.

"If you're bi-polar, please press 1, then 9.

"If you'd like to see one of our pastors, please visit our website at www.bigoldchurch.com.

"If you'd like to make a donation, press 4 to enroll in our handy automatic donation deduction program. Or you may send cash, check, or money order to Mega-Bucks for Mega-Church, P.O. Box 999, Palm Springs, CA 88888. We also accept Visa, MasterCard, American Express, Discover, and Pizza Hut coupons.

By the way, don't forget to catch our weekly *God-O-Mania* pay-per-view worship services, broadcast live via satellite every Sunday at 11:00 A.M. Eastern Standard Time. To be part of this moving, live remote worship experience, contact your local cable company or satellite dish provider.

"Finally if you'd like actual human contact, please understand that our staff is very busy growing the church. If we had to take time to meet with individuals, we wouldn't be the Mega-Church we are today, would we?"

Have you heard messages like this? Are you, as we are, incensed about the unchecked growth of automation and the way it usurps good, old-fashioned personal interaction? If you care about this problem as we do, please give us a call. We'd love to talk about it. Of course if we're not here when you call, you can leave us a message on our deluxe phone machine. And after one week, our phone-machine messages will be forwarded to us by our digital paging service. God bless you, and don't forget to wait for the beep.

The Theological Know-How Dudes, Part *Trois!*

It's the advice column that's sweeping the nation. Seminary professors, theologians, philosophers, and advice columnists are seeking private audiences to solve teleological bugaboos that have troubled them for a lifetime. So go ahead. We have a few minutes before *SportsCenter* comes on. Ask and learn.

Question: My wife and I are really struggling over TV cartoons. Should we let our kids watch them? They seem relatively harmless, but I'm hearing that they are actually dangerous. What do you guys think?

Answer: We'll get to your question in just a moment. Shaggy and Scooby are about to unmask the villain! Aha, it's Mr. Crumpler, the caretaker! We knew it all along! Oh, yeah, now to your question: We're sad to say that we feel TV cartoons are harmful to children. They simply don't provide good life models.

Let's look for a moment at The Flintstones. Fred Flintstone is more of a leader than Barney Rubble. He's taller. He's stronger. He's a better dresser—he wears his tie even when he mows the lawn. And yet when it comes to wives, Barney gets the sweet and attractive Betty with her adorable little giggle. And who does Fred get? Wilma! Mean-spirited, sarcastic, and hollow-eyed. Wilma is the most unlikeable person in cartoon land. She wouldn't even get Dino to play with her if she didn't wear that bone in her hair. But she is Fred's marital "reward" for all his ambition and hard work. That's not an example we want our kids to see.

And what's the deal with Popeye? Here's a guy named after his physical affliction! He has an optical imbalance, which he's clearly aware of. Do Blimpie, Olive Oil, and Bluto really need to call him Popeye? How politically incorrect is that? Do we want our kids going around saying things like, "Hey, I'd like you to meet my friends Repulsive Birthmark and Crooked Yellow Teeth!"? And how about Olive Oil. Poor Popeye is out defending our country as a proud member of the U.S. Navy, and Olive takes up with Bluto. She has no loyalty whatsoever. Of course when Bluto begins to mistreat her, she's shrieking for good old Popeye to save her scrawny neck. So Popeye chokes down a whole can of cold, slimy spinach and pummels Bluto to rescue his fickle girl. She, of course, will turn around and betray him again in the very next episode! Another bad role model for America's children. We'd start endorsing Popeye if they'd have just one episode where Popeye commits Olive to an eating disorder clinic where they force-feed her canned spinach three times a day. Put some meat on her bones and some loyalty in her heart.

We're sorry to present such harsh views on TV cartoons, but this is how we feel. Of course, we might be enticed to change our minds—for a Scooby snack.

Question: I am a twelve-year-old boy. Therefore I belch. The problem is that we recently had Pastor Tompkins over for dinner, and I belched in front of him. Now I'm grounded for a month. I've heard in some cultures it's actually polite to belch. Can you research this and get me un-grounded?

Answer: Sorry, our little twelve-year-old burping buddy. It's simply poor manners to belch in front of Pastor Tompkins. Next time let him belch first.

Question: Hey Theological Know-How Dudes, check this out: Gargantuan! Colossal! Enormous! Gigantic! Behemoth-like! Towering!

Answer: Sure, you talk big.

Question: My wife and I are agonizing about whether to admit to our children that there is no Santa Claus. What's the right thing to do?

> We'd start endorsing Popeye if they'd have just one episode where Popeye commits Olive to an eating disorder clinic where they force-feed her canned spinach three times a day.

Answer: There's no Santa Claus?! No! YOU'RE LYING! YOU'RE LYING! YOU'RE LYING! There is too a Santa Claus! Okay, we're just kidding. We know Santa isn't real. Just don't start questioning the Tooth Fairy, okay? Look, there comes a day when every kid learns the truth about Santa. We both recall that day. We cried and stamped our feet and flung ourselves on the floor. Fortunately, some of our fellow grad students stayed with us in our dorm rooms and helped us endure the bad news.

Question: Your book, especially this Theological Know-How feature, has helped me tremendously. I would like to share it with my family in Guatemala. Any chance that *Snickers From the Front Pew* will be translated into Spanish?

Answer: Yes, we'd like our book to be available for every "Juan." Besides, we think it's a good idea to translate our book into other languages because it loses something in the original English.

Question: Dudes, I'm a teenager battling peer pressure. Peer pressure doesn't rock, dudes. What can I do?

Answer: Don't despair, teen dude. We are, as you might say, hip to your scene, man. And the solution to your peer pressure problem is simple. Become a hermit. They have no peer pressure.

Question: I am troubled by all the sweepstakes, giveaways, and other contest stuff I get in the mail all the time. I keep ordering the magazines and entering the contests, but I never win. Some friends from church say that entering these giveaways is a form of gambling and therefore a sin. But I want to win one of those giant checks, and I promise to use the money for God's glory. Do you guys think I'm gambling?

Answer: Gambling? Perhaps not. But wasting your money? Definitely. To quote our wise Uncle Doyal: "Nobody wins them dad-blasted contests! Them contests is nothing but a rip-off cooked up by them florists unions and some talking woodchucks living under Regis Philbin's garage!" But even if you don't subscribe to Uncle Doyal's viewpoint, consider this: You're most likely not going to get anything for your efforts—except a bunch of insipid entertainment magazines. And how much do you really need to know about Leonardo DiCaprio? He's a skinny guy with lots of vowels in his name. Next topic!

So, next time you get one of those big junk-mail pseudo-giveaway packets in the mail, do what we do. We get a big envelope, paste our picture on the front, and mail it straight to Ed McMahon. And on the front we write, "Hey, Ed! We may have already thrown your stupid contest junk into the trash!"

And a Little Child Shall Mislead Them

One of our favorite jobs at BBC has been leading junior church (motto: "If your kids aren't civilized enough to sit quietly for one hour, send 'em to us!"). Our program embraces kids of almost all ages. Anyone not in a diaper is welcome.

We try to do more than baby-sit our church's beloved little ankle-biters during their time in our special junior church facility (also known as "the unfinished basement"). We aim to give them a solid background in biblical history. And we hold ourselves accountable. At the end of each year, we give the kids paper and pencils, shoot them with tranquilizer darts, and ask them to chronicle what they have learned. (And of course we're kidding about shooting our little curtain-monkeys with tranquilizer darts. It's much easier to mix the stuff in with their Kool-Aid.)

This assignment never fails to elicit some intriguing responses. We're amazed at how much we can teach kids about the Bible in only a few short months. In case you're a little foggy on your biblical history, let our junior church students help you with this complete overview of the Bible, compiled from their essays:

In the beginning which occurred near the start, there was nothing but God, darkness, and some gas. The Bible says, "The Lord thy God is one," but I think He must be a lot older than that. Anyway, God said, "Give me a light!" and someone did. Then God made the world. He split the adam and made Eve. Adam and Eve were naked, but they weren't embarrassed because mirrors hadn't been invented yet. Adam and Eve disobeyed God by eating one bad apple, so they were driven from the Garden of Eden. Not sure what they were driven in though, because they didn't have cars. After that people couldn't live forever and stuff. God said He was just going to let nature take its curse.

Adam and Eve had a son, Cain, who hated his brother as long as he was Abel. Pretty soon all of the early people died off, except for Methuselah, who lived to be like a million or something.

One of the next important people was Noah, who was a good guy, but one of his kids was kind of a ham. Noah built a large boat and put his family and some animals on it. He asked some other people to join him, but they said they would have to take a rain check. Then it poured for forty days and forty nights. Next, Noah sent a dove out to find the Olive Garden and check if it was still under water.

After Noah came Abraham, Isaac, and
Jacob. Jacob was more famous than his
brother, Esau, because Esau sold Jacob his
birthmark in exchange for some pot roast.
Jacob had a son named Joseph who wore a
really loud sports coat. Joseph
thought he was going to be a
great leader, but his brothers
said, "In your dreams, buddy!"

Another important Bible guy
is Moses, whose real name was
Charlton Heston. Moses led the
Israel Lights out of Egypt and
away from the evil Pharaoh after
God sent ten plagues on
Pharaoh's people. These plagues
included frogs, mice, lice,
bowels, and no cable. After God
helped the Israel Lights escape,
He fed them every day with
manicotti. Then He gave them
His top Ten Commandments. These include
don't lie, cheat, smoke, dance, or covet your
neighbor's bottom (the Bible uses a bad word for
bottom that I'm not supposed to say. But my dad
uses it sometimes when he talks about the
President). Anyway, those are pretty much the
only commandments I remember. Oh, yeah, I
just thought of one more: Humor thy father and
thy mother.

One of Moses' best helpers was Joshua,
which is also my cousin Joshua's name.

> Jacob was more
> famous than his
> brother, Esau,
> because Esau
> sold Jacob his
> birthmark in
> exchange for
> some pot roast.

Anyway, Joshua was the first Bible guy to use spies. He sent them to spy on the enemy, but they almost got caught. Luckily, Rahab the Protestant helped them escape. Then Joshua fought the battle of Geritol and the fence fell over on the town.

After Joshua came David. He got to be king by killing a giant with a slingshot. (But when I use my slingshot on my cat, I always get in trouble. P.S.: I didn't kill my cat, but I almost put her eye out.) But David wasn't all good. He did a bad thing by spying on a woman named Sheba while she was taking a bath. (My mom says I shouldn't bother her while she's taking a bath and that I should just go watch cartoons or something.)

David had a son named Solomon who had about 300 wives and 500 porcupines. My teacher says he was wise, but that doesn't sound very wise to me. After Solomon there were a bunch of major league prophets. One of these was Jonah, who was swallowed by a big whale and then barfed up on the shore. There were also some minor league prophets, but I guess we don't have to worry about them.

After the Old Testament came the New Testament. The New Testament is about 2,000 years old, so I'm not sure it should be called "new" anymore. Jesus is the star of the New Testament. He was born in Bethlehem in a barn. (I wish I had been born in a barn, too, because my mom is always saying to me, "Close the door! Were you born in a barn?" It would be nice to say, "As a matter of fact, I was.") Also, Jesus was born on Christmas Day, so I feel a little sorry for Him, having His birthday so close to Christmas and all.

During His life, Jesus had many arguments with sinners like the Pharisees and the Republicans. Jesus also had twelve opossums. The worst one was Judas Asparagus. Judas was so evil that they named a terrible vegetable after him. He later died of apostate cancer.

Jesus was a great man. He healed many leopards and even preached to some Germans on the Mount. But the Republicans and all those guys put Jesus on trial before Pontius the Pilot. Pilot didn't stick up for Jesus. He just washed his hands instead.

Anyway, Jesus died for our sins, then came back to life again. He went up to Heaven but will be back at the end of the Aluminum. His return is foretold in the book of Revolution.

THE END

The Fridges of Madison County: A Compelling Four-Part Family Drama

A few nights ago, we settled in with our wives to watch some high quality network TV. Jedd and I were excited because a Clint Eastwood movie was on. It was called *The Bridges of Madison County*.

Cool, we thought, Clint is going to blow up bridges for the next two hours!

We were deeply disappointed when we discovered Clint would merely be taking pictures of bridges! Where is the fun in that? As the film progressed, our disappointment grew. Not only was the movie boring, it extolled adultery. As we clicked off the set (it was still an hour before *SportsCenter*), we decried the paucity of Hollywood films promoting wholesomeness and virtue.

It's too bad, we agreed, that Clint's attempt at a love story couldn't have been built on a moral foundation. Then it would have been a fine film, even if he didn't get to blow up anything. We started to discuss how we would have approached the making of *Bridges*. We thought that it might be something like this:

Chapter 1

A Good Amana™ Is Hard to Find

"I've never seen such beauty," the tall dark stranger said. "Such exquisite lines. Such proud stature."

Jill felt the color blooming in her cheeks. She smiled and whispered shyly, "Thank you."

Suddenly overcome by passion, the stranger set down the mysterious black leather case he was carrying and reached for the object of his desire—the refrigerator door. "Oh, my!" the stranger gasped as he peaked inside. "Look at the size of that crisper!"

(Who was this statuesque stranger? And why this all-consuming interest in Jill's major appliance? The answers to these and many other questions will be coming soon. In fact, they're only a page away.)

Chapter 2

Double Exposure?

"You must leave now," Jill told the stranger as he admired her refrigerator magnets. "My husband, Clem, and three children will be home soon from the county fair where they're displaying a giant zucchini they grew. Clem will not be happy to find a stranger standing in his kitchen gawking at his refrigerator."

The stranger fought back tears. "All right. I'll go if you insist. But first, you must please grant me one small, innocent picture of your magnificent refrigerator! You see, I'm a photographer for *National Appliances* magazine. I'm doing a feature on great refrigerators and toasters of the Midwest. I have my Yoshika right here in this case, and . . ."

Jill and the stranger froze in horror and turned toward the kitchen window. Clem's pickup was pulling into the driveway!

(Will Jill and the photographer be exposed? See the next page for further developments.)

Chapter 3

Trapped in the Dark Room

"Quick!" Jill ordered the stranger. "Hide in the broom closet!"

Moments later Jill's husband entered the kitchen, smiling. "Darlin', we got the grandest zucchini in the county! Weighed in at forty-eight pounds! Just think of all the zucchini bread you can make from that hummer!"

Suddenly, the proud farmer turned to the broom closet. "Hey, I'll get my camera out of the closet and you can take a picture of me and the kids and the zucchini!" Jill felt her heart thumping as Clem grabbed the doorknob.

The shrieks of pain pierced Jill's ears like an ice pick.

"Those dad-gum kids," her husband muttered, his hand still on the doorknob. "They're teasing the sow again! I gotta go tend to that. We'll have to do the picture later."

(Will the closet photographer escape? And what of the sow? What will be the long-term psychological effects of the teasing she's endured? Watch for the chilling conclusion of *The Fridges of Madison County*—it's only a page away!)

Chapter 4

The Chilling Finale

"You must leave immediately!" Jill told the stranger in the broom closet. "You can go out the front while Clem is out back assisting the sow."

"Come with me," the dark man implored. "Leave this bucolic world and help me capture breathtaking appliances, on film, of course."

Jill teetered on the brink of indecision. She thought of the stranger, of Clem, the zucchini, her children, the sow. Perhaps . . . nah, she thought. She faced the stranger. "I'm sorry. I can't go with you. Please leave now. And take your Yoshika with you."

"All right. I'll go if you insist. But first, you must please grant me one small, innocent picture of your magnificent refrigerator!

Jill smiled wistfully as she watched the stranger walk down her driveway. She wondered about the life he could have offered her. But as she heard her grunting husband carrying the zucchini into the kitchen, she knew her place was right here where she would have all the love (and all the zucchini bread) she could ever ask for.

The End

Bradd knew something was awry when he saw
a pirate exiting our church with fried chicken
on his breath and Dad's gym bag in his hand.

By Hook or by Crook

Our church sat right across the street from Broomfield Elementary School, for which our brother Bradd was extremely grateful. That meant that every school day at lunch time he could briefly escape from the madness that was grade school, slip into the church basement, and enjoy his meal in peace. No food fights. No sixth-grade hooligans shaking him down for his lunch money. And no having to choke down fare such as refried okra surprise. Bradd liked to put it this way: "I'm not eating a bunch of sorry school-made slop while sitting in a loud cafeteria with a bunch of losers."

Our mom accommodated Bradd's yen for a quiet, home-cooked midday repast by preparing a sack lunch for him each morning. On his way to school, Bradd would store his bounty in the church refrigerator where it would wait for him, chilled to exactly forty-two degrees Fahrenheit. At precisely 11:25 A.M. each day, Bradd would sprint across the street, snag his bag, sit at Dad's desk, and flirt with the sin of gluttony.

Bradd enjoyed his home-cooked respites for most of his grade-school career. Then in fifth grade, disaster struck. One cloudy Wednesday, Bradd entered the church just as an oddly dressed man was exiting. He wore a patch over his left eye, a billowy white shirt with crescent-shaped stains under both arms, and snug black trousers. In his left hand, he carried a green gym bag.

"G-day, Matey! God loves ye!" he greeted Bradd, as he wiped his mouth on his sleeve.

Bradd offered the curious stranger his standard reply: "Whatever."

Stepping inside the church, Bradd could almost smell the leftover fried chicken that would be his Wednesday feast. Actually, he did more than almost smell it because as he descended the stairs to the basement he saw that they were littered with chicken bones.

Frantic, Bradd sprinted to the refrigerator. Lying at the base of the old Amana was a grease-spotted brown paper bag crumpled like a giant spit wad. Lovingly, Bradd smoothed out the bag and looked inside. Even the brownie had been eaten! All that remained was a half-gnawed carrot stick.

Bradd put his hands on the refrigerator to steady himself. "Breathe," he told himself. "It's only a few pieces of chicken. Crispy, flavorful, spiced-to-perfection, and a rich, creamy brownie.

"AAAARRRRRRRRRGGGHHHH!"

Our brother's cry of anguish alerted Dad, who was in the basement bathroom, searching for sermon illustrations in the sports section of the *Broomfield Bulletin*. He hurried to Bradd's side. "What's wrong, Bud?" he asked.

"Some lousy pirate stole my lunch!" Bradd squealed.

"A pirate?"

"Yeah. A stinkin' pirate. With a bushy, black beard and a patch over his left eye. Poofy shirt. The whole bit."

Dad grinned. "Did this scalawag who pilfered your lunch also have a peg leg and a parrot?"

"Keep grinning, Dad. He stole your gym bag too."

Dad pounded his right fist into his palm. "That's an outrage! I'll see that he's clapped in irons. I'll make him walk the plank, I will!"

With that, Dad and Bradd climbed aboard the Good Ship Hafer (also known as our 1964 Rambler™) and began the chase. Drawing on their vast knowledge of pirate lore, they surmised that the lunch-grabbing buccaneer might have a hankering for a bottle o' rum after his meal. So they began their search of Broomfield's twenty-one bars.

They saw him coming out of bar number three, the Mint Tulip. "That's him! Starboard side, dead ahead!" Bradd yelled, as Captain Crook stumbled out of the bar.

"Avast, there, Matey!" Dad called.

The pirate turned, and squinted at Dad and Bradd with his good eye.

"That's a nice gym bag you have there, Mate," Dad said cheerfully.

"Why," the pirate stammered, "Thank-ee."

"You know how I know it's such a nice bag?" Dad said, keeping his voice strong and steady.

"Why is that Cap'n?"

"Because it's mine."

The pirate nervously probed a finger under his eye-patch and scratched fervently. Then absent-mindedly he switched the patch from his left eye to his right.

"Did you see that, Dad?" Bradd screamed. "He's not even a real one-eyed pirate!"

"Well, I did have a stye a while back," Captain Crook offered weakly. "I guess the ointment took care of it. Aye, that must have been what happened."

"You're going to need more than ointment if you don't give me back my gym bag," Dad said evenly.

"I swear on a dead man's chest, Matey. This is my bag. My booty."

"If you don't drop that booty, I'm going to kick yours. I'm going to trim your sails. Scuttle your hull."

The pirate eyed Dad—all 6'2", 275 pounds of him. He thought for a moment, then dropped the bag on the sidewalk, where it clanked heavily, like a sack full of axe heads. Puzzled, Dad unzipped the bag. He shook his head and began to remove items. A stapler, a calculator, a praying hands letter opener, a pair of lead angel bookends, an Adam and Eve paperweight.

Dad glared at Captain Crook.

"Those are all mine," came the hasty reply. "A pirate can never have too many office supplies."

Dad turned over the stapler and revealed a red label with raised white capital letters: PROPERTY OF BROOMFIELD BAPTIST CHURCH.

"Well, shiver me timbers!" the pirate stammered.

Dad smiled. "Tell you what I'm gonna do, Blackbeard." He reached into his pocket for some change. "Here are a couple doubloons. I want you to go over to that phone booth up the street and call the police and turn yourself in. The number is on the phone. When the nice police dispatcher answers, I want you to say, 'Ahoy, I'm a thievin' pirate who steals food from children and supplies from a church. I need to spend some time in the brig.' And while you're in the brig, I suggest you think about repenting, Matey."

"Brig?" the pirate said.

"Aw," Bradd muttered disgustedly, "he doesn't even know the lingo. Do you know what 'Davey Jones' locker' means, you chicken-chomping loser?"

"Bradd," Dad corrected, "I'll handle this."

Dad stared at the pirate the way a vegetarian looks at a plate of steak tartare.

Slowly, Captain Crook ambled to the phone booth. He made the call and waited a few minutes. Soon Officer Nutter, one of Dad's weightlifting buddies, arrived. "Time to set sail for Broomfield County Jail, Mr. Pirate," he said cheerfully. "But cheer up, we're showing *Peter Pan* tonight on the video." With that Officer Nutter placed his beefy arm around Captain Crook's shoulder and led him away.

"Hey Pastor," he called over his shoulder, "I got my bench press up to 280 yesterday!"

The pirate eyed Dad—all 6'2", 275 pounds of him. He thought for a moment, then dropped the bag on the sidewalk, where it clanked heavily, like a sack full of axe heads.

205

"Keep it up and someday you'll be able to lift a whole treasure chest," Dad hollered after him.

"Dad," Bradd said, "this was kinda fun, but I still didn't get to eat. Do you think you could take me to lunch?"

Dad patted Bradd's head. "Sure, where would you like to go?"

"Anywhere but Long John Silver's!"

Searching for "Mr. Right"

As we've noted elsewhere in this book, being pastor's kids meant we were often called upon to complete multitudes of menial tasks: unclogging the baptistry, buffing the pews, fumigating the nursery, changing the church van's oil, and, of course, the annual renting of the Steam-O-Matic and trying to get grape Kool-Aid stains out of the fellowship area carpet.

However, as we grew into our awkward teen years, we were occasionally drafted for real spiritual/intellectual work—work that would allow us to unbushel our lights and let them shine for all the congregation (or at least the elders) to see. We were and are (and we try not to say this pridefully) members of the search committee! That's right, whenever the church needed a part-time secretary or interim choir director, we were there, sitting on one side of a faux-wood folding table, staring down the candidates with the rest of the poor committee members who sacrificed a night of Must-See TV to do the Lord's work.

Usually, the interviews were very simple:

"So, Ms. Shyrobin, you say you've been singing in the shower your entire life?"

"Yeah. That's right."

"And you understand that this job pays $2.65 per hour and the piano bench has one wobbly leg?"

"Yeah. I'm cool with that."

"Congratulations, Ms. Choir Director!"

One interview, though, was unlike all the others. A few years ago, Broomfield Baptist Church decided it needed a "Full-Time Youth Professional," so we placed ads in youth publications and put up flyers at the YMCA. How the applications poured in! It's amazing how many people are eager for a job that pays twelve grand a year, plus gas allowance.

Our committee scrutinized each application, eliminating some for various reasons (e.g., being written in crayon or having heart-dots over each letter "i.") When we had picked the elite of the elite, we set up an evening-long session of interviews.

We looked forward to interviewing the candidates, as we sat at the table with the rest of the committee: Chet the elder, Dave the elder, Backbeat Florence the organist, and Berton the Sunday school superintendent. We thought it would be fun to chat with the candidates, all of them recent Bible college graduates. Get to know them as people. Share a few jokes. Maybe go out for pizza when it was all done.

But something strange happened as the first candidate sat down in one of BBC's deluxe metal folding chairs. Assuming they were facing a bright, Bible-college-educated intellectual, the other search' committee members explored the recesses of their intellects for something to impress the candidate. It was as if they were thinking, "Okay, we may be from the little town of Broomfield and have hay in our hair and manure on our boots, but we can dissect Habakkuk with the best of them!"

At first, we were amused by our colleagues' efforts to impress. Chet the elder opened the interview by asking candidate Skip, an eager-faced redhead, "Could you please describe for us your hermeneutical demeanor?"

We nearly spit out our beverages at that one. We've always held that a man should never describe his hermeneutical demeanor in mixed company. After a while though, our surprise and amusement turned to plain old boredom.

To us, the evening sounded like this:

"Blah, blah, blah, blah, post-Hegelian phenomenology yada, yada, yada hypotheses of the religious demographers, mumbo-jumbo, mumbo-jumbo antinomian proclivities, yakety-yak-yak-yak ex nihilo? You wanna talk ex nihilo! Blather, blather, blather, dynamic-equivalent textual criticism, yabba-dabba-dooooooo!"

We were shaken from our coma-like state by Dave the elder: "Well, you two pastor's sons have been awfully quiet this evening. May I remind you that Mike Oswalt here is our last candidate of the night? Don't you have anything to ask him? Our ninety minutes with him are almost up. But we haven't covered the Apostle John's rebuttal of the Gnostics yet. Care to pick up that ball and run with it?"

We looked at poor Mike Oswalt, a plump guy with a blonde crew-cut and skin the color of watermelon flesh. Sweat was trickling down both sides of his face. His shoulders were slumped. He looked, as Chet the Elder liked to say when he wasn't trying to impress people, "like he's done been rode hard and put away wet."

We looked at poor Mike Oswalt, a plump guy with a blonde crew-cut and skin the color of watermelon flesh. Sweat was trickling down both sides of his face. His shoulders were slumped.

"Mister Chairman Chet," Todd began, trying to raise his eyelids from their Garfield half-mast level, "we do indeed have a few questions to ask Mr. Oswalt."

All the members of the committee leaned forward in their chairs, anticipating the theological fastballs we would attempt to hurl past young Mike. Mike stared at us, looking frightened—like a bunny cornered by a rabid jackal.

"Well, Mister Oswalt," Todd continued, "I'd like to know something of your capabilities when it comes to placing your hand under your armpit and squeezing out a camp song or two."

The fear fled from Mike's eyes, and the trace of a smile formed around his pudgy lips. "I can do eighty-seven armpit tunes, sir," he said proudly. "It'll be eighty-eight when I perfect 'God Told Noah to Build an Arky-Arky!'"

Todd nodded approvingly. "Can I assume, then, Mister Oswalt, that you can also belch the entire alphabet?"

Mike cleared his throat. "That would be correct, sir. If anyone has a liter of root beer, I'd be happy to demonstrate."

Todd shuffled some papers. "That won't be necessary, Mister Oswalt. I'm through here. Your witness, Jedd."

Jedd stroked his chin thoughtfully. "I have just one question of Mister Oswalt."

"Can you tell me, precisely, how many marshmallows you can cram into your mouth and still enunciate the words 'chubby bunny?'"

"Would that be the mini marshmallows, sir, or the jumbos?"

Jedd nibbled on his pencil. "Let us say for the sake of argument the minis."

"Eighty-nine sir."

We looked at each other and said, nearly, in unison, "Congratulations Mr. New Youth Pastor, you da MAN!"

There was a bit of harrumphing among the other members of the search committee, but eventually Chet the elder stood and spoke, in his normal persona: "Well, there, Mister Oswalt, on accounta the Hafer boys have taken a likin' to ya, we'd like to offer you the, uh, full-time Youth Professional job."

Much hand shaking and "Bless ya, Brother"-ing followed.

We congratulated Mike and exited the church with a clear sense of mission accomplished and a vague craving for miniature marshmallows.

Dad's robe was olive green (minus the pimento)
and was certainly large enough to cover
an adult male, as long as that male
was a *jockey*.

The Robe Less Traveled

Christmas time at Broomfield Baptist Church always means one thing: The Annual All-Church Christmas Program, also known as "The Poorly Contrived Debacle With Barely-Tolerable Music."

One particularly memorable year, Betty Eunice, the choir director, decided to produce a program titled *Away in a Manger*. On November first, she proudly and carefully arranged the letters on our outdoor sign. We assumed she wanted to give people plenty of advance warning (oops, we mean notice about the program).

Unfortunately, her foresight gave our brother Chadd too much time to stare at the sign:

Come One, Come All

to Broomfield Baptist Church's
Christmas presentation of
AWAY IN A MANGER!

After carefully evaluating the sign for a week, Chadd walked to the church late one night and removed an "A" and an "M" from the board. Then he stood back to admire his work. AWAY IN A MANGER! was now AWAY IN ANGER!

The sign stayed that way until the morning of the program. We were sure that Betty Eunice must not have seen the change or someone would have experienced grief and woe of Old Testament proportions. As for the people who saw the NCV (New Chadd Version) sign, the title must have intrigued them because on that fateful December day Broomfield Baptist Church was packed to the rafters with an eager standing-room-only crowd.

That year our dad was fortunate enough to be chosen to play the prophet Isaiah, a role that suited him to a "t." His job in the program was to walk to the podium and foretell the Christmas story, wearing a robe fit for an Old Testament important person.

During the first three weeks of December, all the rest of the cast members worked diligently on their costumes, striving to achieve painstaking biblical/historical accuracy. They bejeweled their headdresses. They wove their own sandals. They fashioned tunics or togas or whatever they call them from authentic goat skin (Well, it certainly *looked* authentic).

As for our dad's preparation, well, let's just say that the first three weeks of December comprised the crucial part of the National Football League season. Costumes were not part of his consciousness unless they had last names and numbers on them and belonged to the Denver Broncos.

However, to his credit, we must point out that Dad put several moments of thought into his costume as he rolled out of bed on the morning of the presentation. He shucked the pillow case off his pillow and wrapped it around his head, securing it with his favorite tie (the blue and white checked number with the little yellow rocking horsies). Then he gazed into his bedroom mirror and said, "Behold, an authentic Old Testament prophet turban!"

For the finishing touch, he threw on "the robe." The robe is famous in our family. Until that day, it was not famous beyond our family because Mom decreed that it was never (under any circumstances) to be worn outside the house.

The robe was olive-green (minus the pimento) and was certainly large enough to cover an adult male, as long as that male was a jockey. On a large former semi-professional football player, the robe was like a tea cozy on a keg of root beer. We can only imagine the draft Dad felt when he stepped into the crisp December air and walked to the church that morning.

Betty Eunice nearly had a heart attack when she saw Dad waiting backstage.

"Pastor Hafer!" she gasped. "Where's your costume? And what is that thing on your head? Has one of your awful children played another joke on you?"

Dad frowned and adjusted his authentic pillow-case turban. "This is my costume," he announced, punctuating the words with his signature tone of pastoral authority. Poor Betty Eunice was decidedly outgunned.

"Oh, my! Oh, my! Oh, my!" said Betty Eunice, holding on to a cardboard oxen for support.

Dad shrugged his massive shoulders, adjusted the mini-robe, and took his place at stage left (also known as the secretary's office).

A hush fell over the congregation as a crimson-faced Betty Eunice stepped to the microphone, fanning herself with a bulletin. "We are, uh, proud, to present to you, uh, our Christmas program today. It's called *Away in a Manger*. God help us all."

Then she sat down in the front pew and began to weep softly.

Dad, taking that as his cue, emerged from stage left and thundered to the podium. Chadd held his breath. His new girlfriend, Sarah, had come all the way from Maryland to visit for Christmas. Her eyes grew as big as pies when she saw Dad's enormous, tree-trunk thighs—almost all of them.

She leaned over and whispered to Chadd, "Hey, is that your dad or a retired member of The Power Team?"

Chadd's eyes were fixed on the major prophet before him. "Who?" he said absently.

"The huge guy in the little robe, Chadd! The guy reading from the scroll? Is that your dad?"

Chadd drew a long, slow breath. He looked Sarah directly in the eye. "No. No. That's not my dad. My dad is sick today. He's not here. He's not anywhere near here."

Somewhere, probably over at the Hanson farm, a rooster crowed.

Fortunately, Dad's part was over quickly. After the opening scene, he stepped down from the podium, tossed his scroll to Betty Eunice, and lumbered to the back of the sanctuary where Mom was frantically waving a T-shirt and an extra-large pair of sweat pants. Then he sat in a back pew and enjoyed the rest of the program. He even gave a solo standing ovation to Chet the elder after his tuba solo.

When the program was over (and the plastic baby Jesus was returned safely to the nursery, where he was

known as G.I. Joe), the church began buzzing about
the robe. A few of the elders teased Dad about his
attire, saying that the real prophet Isaiah was probably
taking some razzing in Heaven right about then.

"Hey, Pastor Del," Dave the elder said, "I'm glad
your part didn't call for you to bend over. You woulda
been arrested!"

Dad was unmoved by the chiding. He began to hold
court in the fellowship area, explaining that his costume
was authentic. "Old Testament prophets didn't make a
lot of money," he noted. "They couldn't afford a lot of
material for their clothes. Jeremiah, in fact, often wore
nothing but a loincloth and a calfskin knee brace."

The elders nodded in bewildered agreement. Chadd,
however, was livid. "Hey, Dad," he said, "I have a
prophecy for you: If you ever wear that robe in public
again, me and the rest of the family are converting to
another religion and moving to Idaho! Also, I told my
new girlfriend you weren't my dad, so could you please
not come home till she goes back to Maryland?"

Dad stared at Chadd. Then he picked up the robe,
stuffed it into the pocket of his sweats, and went
"away in anger."

Chadd and Dad eventually reconciled over the
event, although Sarah took an early flight back to
Maryland and never communicated with Chadd again.

And there were two more bits of fall-out from that
fateful Sunday. Betty Eunice decreed that from that
point on, all Christmas programs were to be "non-
prophet" affairs. But just to be on the safe side, Mom
cut up the robe and made it into two oven mitts—
rather small ones.

One afternoon we found Dad's living room chair encircled by Boy Scouts. Dad was proclaiming to them, "So, to put Paul's words in terms you can understand: When I was a Cub Scout, I spoke and thought as a Cub Scout. But when I became an Eagle Scout, I put away Cub Scout things."

The Witnessing Protection Program

Few things scare our mom. After all, she's married to a pastor and has raised four energetic boys who loved to play with fire and preferred pets caught in the wild to those carefully selected at Pet City. It wasn't uncommon for her to hear things like, "Mom, be careful when you go out to water the lawn. Snakey's in the window well. He's our new pet rattler. But don't worry; he's just a baby. His venom can't kill you yet—just makes you get a fever and maybe barf."

Or, "Mom, when you put the empty bottles in the milk box, be careful to not crush our new pet, Mister Hairy Spider. And, hey, could you tell us whether he's a tarantula or a wolf spider?"

Mom does fear one thing though: door-to-door missionaries representing various religious disorders. Terror has always seized her when the doorbell rings and it's not the Avon lady or some church folk bringing a pie. Mom has good reason to be afraid. She is too nice for her own good, and she knows it. She's always been a sucker for traveling salespeople whether they are peddling vitamins, "revolutionary" vacuums, or spiritual peace.

Mom worried that if some proselytizer ever engaged her in conversation, Dad would come home to hear her confess, "I'm so sorry, honey, but I joined Swami Suchabanana's Church of Enlightenment today. His missionaries were so cute in their little turbans that I just couldn't resist."

Thus, to protect herself from her own kindness, Mom has a system whenever the doorbell rings. First, she peeks through the curtains. If she spots one or more strangers holding pamphlets, she hits the floor and scoots to the kitchen like a World War II commando. Next she signals us to be quiet and turn off all electronic devices. Then we all hold our breath and wait for the missionaries to leave our porch and go next door to speak to the neighbors.

Our dad, on the other hand, has always welcomed any and all doorstep visitors. He feels slighted that he gets to preach only three times a week, and thus is delighted for additional opportunities to practice his craft. And he loves a good spiritual debate almost as much as a forty-minute, seven-point sermon. Dad is unbiased as to his encounters as well. Whether the visitor is a census taker or an insurance peddler, Dad feels no qualms about engaging him or her in a rousing session of ecclesiastical give-and-take.

One afternoon we came home to find Dad's living room chair encircled by Boy Scouts. Dad was proclaiming to them, "So, to put Paul's words in terms you can understand: When I was a Cub Scout, I spoke and thought as a Cub Scout. But when I became an Eagle Scout, I put away Cub Scout things."

A pack of Girl Scouts faced a similar lesson: "Okay, then, let's say that these Thin Mints represent Jesus' disciples, and these Oatmeal Scotchies are the Pharisees."

Dad was even more daunting when it came to those visitors who were intent upon persuading us to join a different religious faith. He saw these folks as wolves set on devouring his small but beloved flock. He would begin the interrogation by asking if they spoke classical Greek. Then he would shake his head in disappointment when they said no. To him that was tantamount to admitting, "No, we don't bathe regularly or take a daily multi-vitamin."

"How can you expect to do a thorough exegetical contrast between our two belief systems if you can't conjugate a simple intransitive Greek predicate?" he would ask incredulously. At this point, the missionaries usually asked to use our bathroom or suddenly remembered an important haircut appointment.

Though we could never prove it, we believed that the veteran missionaries sometimes sent their trainees to our place to test their mettle. "Go visit that house next to the Broomfield Baptist Church," they'd tell their young charges. "If you can get through to that guy, you will be ready for an apostolic ministry!"

We'll never forget Deena and Wally, two unsuspecting rookie envoys from the Church of the Partially Leavened Bread who came by one evening. Dad was watching *Monday Night Football* but welcomed an interruption from Deena and Wally, especially when they confessed they were Oakland Raiders fans. Dad quickly explained to them how the weak special teams and inconsistency at quarterback made the Raiders a mediocre outfit.

"But we like their helmets," Deena protested.

Dad snorted, "Come now, Deena, helmet logos are purely marketing gimmicks. It's defense and a well conceived, ball-control-oriented offensive game plan that wins championships."

At this point, Wally jumped in and asked if Dad would read "some of our literature." He handed Dad a limp pamphlet.

"Tell you what," Dad smiled, "I'll be glad to read your pamphlet if you'll read something for me."

"Uh . . . okay," Wally said, looking as if he'd just agreed to donate some brain tissue.

Dad sprinted to his study and returned with a three-ring binder the size of Rhode Island (which isn't an island, by the way, and we find that disturbing). "This is a position paper I wrote on the inerrancy of the Bible," he announced. "I originally penned it in Greek and Aramaic, but I think you'll be more comfortable with this condensed and simplified English version. You two read this over and come back next Monday. We can discuss it while we watch the Broncos stampede your Raiders."

Deena and Wally ejected from their places on the couch as if they'd been goosed by Captain Hook. They mumbled that they'd "try to make it by" and headed for their ten-speeds.

"Hey," Dad called after them, "what do you use to lube your bike chains?"

"I think 3-in-1 oil," Wally replied hesitantly.

The Reverend Hafer shook his head again. "No good, Wally. Wrong viscosity for nice bikes like those. Use Tri-Flow instead and see if you don't get a smoother ride."

"Okay," Wally said obediently.

Then the twosome peddled away as if they were doing a sprint leg of the Tour de France. Wally lagged behind, weighed down by the inerrancy tome bulging from his backpack.

"See you next week!" Dad yelled. "And by the way, I'm not just a pastor; I also sell insurance. Go, Broncos!"

Wally tried to speed up and lost his balance. He hit Mabel Rodgers' aspen tree head on. But without looking back, he adjusted his backpack and limped off into the night.

So, Wally, if you're reading this, please come back to our house. We still have your bike. Dad straightened the handlebars and lubed it for you. He also inflated the tires to the ideal pressure and adjusted your seat. He says you were riding too low for a man of your height, body type, and posture.

One more thing, Wally. Dad would also like to chat with you "for just a few minutes" about formal and dynamic equivalence Bible translations and their bearing on post-Chalcedonian antinomianism. So y'all come back now, ya hear?

The only Hafer brother who even tolerated
Mom's guild meetings was Bradd, who was
enticed by the gorge-fest. "Mom and those guild
chicks just yap away," he would say. "One time I
ate three pieces of pie and nine brownies, and
no one was the wiser."

Crying Over Spilled Beans

One peaceful Saturday morning, Jedd, then age six, was playing his favorite game: G.I. Joe versus New Testament disciple wrestling. In these contests, a plastic talking G.I. Joe figure (with lifelike hair and kung-fu grip) would battle it out with one of Mom's Sunday school flannel-graph disciples atop a couch cushion that served as the wrestling ring.

In this particular contest, Bartholomew the Disciple was working on converting G. I. Joe into a mangled heap of plastic and lifelike hair.

"You think you're tough just because you're three-dimensional, Joe?" Bartholomew taunted, "Well, take this!" Bartholomew slashed at Joe, giving him a nasty, though invisible, papercut.

"Jedd," Mom interrupted, showing little or no respect for military maneuvers, "we've got to get on the road. Hurry and put away your toys and my disciple."

"Mom," Jedd challenged (We've found that soldiering games often cause young males to act foolishly in the face of danger.) "Bartholomew is Jesus' disciple, not yours. You didn't live in Bible times and you don't know a thing about fishing or tax collecting."

Mom, who apparently was feeling pretty merciful, flashed him one of her signature "don't mess with me" smiles. "Now come along, you little scamp," she said. "Get moving before you make me late to my meeting!"

Jedd was in the car before he had time to think about the significance of the words "my meeting." But as the Hafer Chrysler Monstrosity pulled out of the driveway, Jedd experienced an epiphany. He and Mom were on their way to the monthly gathering of the Broomfield Baptist Church Women's Guild!

Jedd had heard many tales of guild grief and woe from his brothers, who had endured many a guild luncheon when they were younger, more naive, and easier to bully. "It's horrible!" they had lamented. "Dozens of ladies, coated with makeup and perfume, smother you with bear hugs and pinch the business out of your cheeks. Then they sing songs in really high voices and stuff you full of bean casserole. Avoid the guild at all cost."

So as horror filled his six-year-old brain, Jedd began to beg Mom: "Do I have to go to this thing? Couldn't we go to the dentist instead?"

"You certainly do have to go, young man," Mom chided. "Your Dad and brothers are at Todd's track meet today. You didn't want to go, remember?"

Jedd slumped in his seat, filled with despair and dread. The only Hafer brother who even remotely tolerated the guild was Bradd, who quite frankly was enticed by the gorge-fest, a never-violated tradition for all church women's meetings. Bradd returned one Saturday with a sly grin pasted on his face. After much prying from his three siblings, Bradd finally admitted his secret.

"Mom and those guild chicks just yap away for most of the meeting," he explained. "They don't even pay attention when the dessert is served! I ate three pieces of pie and nine brownies, and no one was the wiser." Jedd, remembering his brother's remarks, took comfort. As soon as he and Mom had cleared the door, he located the brownies and began to fill his pockets and cheeks.

Things seemed to be looking up until Mrs. Oppelmeister trotted to the podium to introduce the speaker. "You all know our speaker for today," she beamed. "It's Cherie Hafer, Pastor Hafer's better half! Actually, when you realize how big Pastor Hafer is," she continued, "Cherie is more like his better fourth." As the room filled with snickers, Mom strolled to the podium, stopping to wink at Jedd on the way up. It was then that it hit him—brownie tumbling from his mouth. Mom was about to use him as a patsy— someone to be the subject of an "Illustration Humiliation."

We Hafer brothers had grown accustomed to Dad using our every boneheaded word and deed to spice up his sermons. But Mom's use of our blunders still made us wince. After all, she was the one who potty-trained us, gave us baths, and did our laundry.

Jedd steeled himself for the worst. But to his amazement, none of the stories that spilled from

Mom's lips were about him. They were all about Dad and his brothers.

Mom shared the time Bradd brought home the "pretty kitty" that was in fact a skunk, and how Chadd once mistook the tuba of a visiting band for a golden toilet.

She told about Dad catching the dryer on fire while trying to fix it with a can of WD-40 and sandpaper. And about the day a flu-stricken Todd threw up on a Gideon Bible representative.

She waxed eloquently as she described the Christmas pageant where Chadd played the part of the innkeeper, cheerfully telling Mary and Joseph, "Oh, sure, there's plenty of room in my inn! Would you like a smoking or non-smoking room?"

After each story, Jedd would look at all the ladies around him and wag his head from side to side, as if to say, "They're all dumb but me!"

Then just as Mom launched into a tale about the time Dad forgot his glasses before a trip to the supermarket and purchased prune juice for communion, a clamor arose from the back of the auditorium. Everyone turned to see Dad, Todd, Chadd, and Bradd, standing in the doorway, dripping wet and hopping mad.

The track meet had been rained out, so they had come to support Mom in her speaking endeavor. They had been standing there dripping for quite a while before some of the women in the back noticed the smell of wet guys and began passing the word that their guild meeting had been infiltrated.

Mom, sensing trouble, squelched the prune juice saga and closed in prayer.

When the Hafer family arrived home, tension filled the air. Everyone glared at Mom, including G.I. Joe and Bartholomew the fighting disciple.

Dad quickly assumed the role of spokesperson for the collective Hafer male outrage. "I hope you're happy," he began. "You have humiliated us, all for the sake of cheap entertainment. We are your family, not mere illustration fodder," he roared.

"Technically, Dad," Todd interjected. "you are the *Fodder* and Mom is the *Mudder.*"

Everyone spoke in unison. "Shut up, Todd!"

Dad then returned to his remarks. "How could you do this to us? You must protect the sanctity and privacy of this family."

Mom stated her case clearly and confidently. "How about all those cracks you regularly make about my pot roast, Pastor Hafer? Do you remember that?"

"Oh, but that's different" Dad responded. "I'm a trained professional. I've been to seminary. When you let an untrained person use family members as illustrations, it's like giving a crossbow to an orangutan."

The next day during his sermon, Dad drove home his point by using Mom's misuse of illustrations as an illustration! That definitely taught her a lesson. Although to this day, none of us is sure what lesson it was.

From Here "Toe" Eternity

We met Allison in California a few years ago, but we see people like her almost everywhere we go. Her brown eyes were downcast, her shoulders hunched, her head bowed, and her arms crossed tightly across her chest, as if she were trying to give herself a hug. Maybe she thought nobody else would.

When we meet the Allisons of the world, we come to realize that they don't understand their value and importance in life. They don't realize their roles as God's extraordinary works of art. We know what these people need to hear. And just in case you're like Allison or know someone who is, we'd like you to hear what she heard.

Todd's Little Toe Story

A few years ago, I was running late to a speaking gig. I rushed through my morning routine, saddened that I wouldn't have time to lather, rinse, and repeat in the shower. Ah, yes, the shower. It would be my downfall—literally.

As I bounded from the shower that frantic morn, eager to look in the mirror and see if I could bypass shaving, I smashed my right baby toe against the shower's hard, cold, unforgiving steel bottom rim.

Have you ever tried to kick a bowling ball with your bare foot? If so, stop listening and immediately seek professional help. If not, use your imagination as I describe the sensation. My toe erupted with sparks of pain, as if someone had detonated a tiny load of toe dynamite in there.

It was like Jerry Springer— an ever-present distress that showed no sign of going away any time soon.

I didn't swear, but I did scream, "Ah-mano-woo-weeeeeeeee!" which I believe is Cherokee for "Your mother's plantar warts bring great dishonor to our village."

Then in panic, I looked down at my toe. It was throbbing and as red as a stop sign. I could almost see the pain radiating from it. I paused, bit my lower lip, and waited for the agony to subside. It didn't. It was like Jerry Springer—an ever-present distress that showed no sign of going away any time soon.

As I limped about and continued to get ready, the pain slithered from my toe to my foot, then my ankle, knee, and hip. I realized I was favoring my left leg, and this was throwing my body out of balance. Finally with great effort, I managed to put on everything but my sleek Italian leather shoes which my wife picked out for me. I tried to ease my foot into the first shoe, but my toe wouldn't cooperate. It couldn't bear the pain and strain of being pressed, anvil-like, between its toe buddies and the unforgiving shoe leather.

This was a true case of toe jam.

Thus I was forced to wear my black Air Jordan high-tops with my navy blue suit. I looked like an escaped mental patient—or a rapper.

By the time I hobbled to the podium to address the Christian Bass Fishers, the pain had spread to my back, neck, and head. (By the way, the bass fishers were Christians; I cannot speak for the bass themselves.)

Anyway, my discomfort prevented me from concentrating on my speech, and I stunk up the place like a three-day-old carp. They didn't even like my joke about the man with the defective bobber.

All this because of an injury to one three-quarter-inch toe. Actually, it was three-quarters of an inch before the accident. It's only a half-inch now. I was reminded of my high school buddy Kurt Wheeler, who accidentally shot off his little toe while cleaning his .22. He required physical therapy to relearn how to walk properly.

"You never realize how much you need a little toe until it's gone," Kurt used to say. Then he'd add, "Anybody wanna go duck hunting?"

Nobody ever did.

I pictured Kurt's gait after the toe shot. Even with lots of therapy, he couldn't run as quickly or smoothly as before.

One can derive two lessons from "Todd's Little Toe Story." First, be careful entering and exiting your shower.

More importantly, remember that Christ's body needs all its parts to function effectively and without pain. The people who are the hands may feel honored because they get to wave, eat, clap, and shake with foreign dignitaries. So maybe if you're a little toe, you feel inferior when compared to the larger, more visible parts.

But the body needs you. Without you, its balance is thrown off kilter. And other parts begin to hurt as they try to compensate for your absence. Don't forget that every part of the body is important as we run this race called life. So get out there Allison (or whatever your name is) and toe the line.

A Third Not-Too-Terrible Parable

Okay, this one doesn't have a monk in it, but we hope it will make its point nonetheless.

The Pedicurist's Plea

A thirty-ish pedicurist named Nancy was walking through a meadow on a clear, Thursday afternoon. As she strolled, she marveled at the grandeur of creation all around her. The meadow teemed with life and beauty. She noticed a plethora of plant life, an abundance of animal life, and a myriad of minerals.

She saw approximately a thousand hills, each occupied by cattle. She was overcome with admiration for the God that created and owned it all. "God," she said aloud, "I am awed by your creation. All of this is yours—the earth, the sky, the water—and all the life contained therein. You must laugh at humanity's view of riches. Not even the richest person alive could compare to You."

God's voice rumbled down from the heavens. "You are correct, my daughter. Human riches pale next to mine."

"Yes, they do," Nancy said emphatically. "We place such high value on millionaires down here, but to you what is a million dollars?"

God laughed. "To me a million dollars is but a penny!"

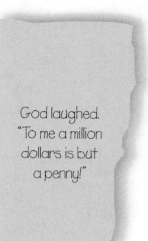

God laughed. "To me a million dollars is but a penny!"

"That is so cool," Nancy cried. Then she strolled and thought some more. She noticed the sun slowly sinking in the western sky. "God," she called, "the day is slipping away down here. It will be night soon. Then it will be another day. But what is the passing of time to you? We pay much attention to the days, weeks, months, and years. We mark them on our calendars. We bemoan how quickly they pass us by. But you must view time differently—even large chunks of time. I mean, to one who is eternal, what is a million years?"

God chuckled again, "My daughter, to me a million years is but a second."

"Wow!" Nancy marveled. "A million dollars is like a penny to you, and a million years is like a second! What a concept!"

Then Nancy grew quiet. She began to think. "God," she asked hopefully, "may I have a penny?"

"Sure," God replied, "in a second!"

Items to Ponder and Amuse Yourself with While You Wait for Snickers II

We're confused by the information coming out of the Pentagon. There seem to be five sides to every story.

If the bald eagle is our national bird, shouldn't some of our tax dollars go to buying the poor thing a toupé?

Edgar Allen Poe was a raven lunatic.

We were saddened to hear that for financial reasons Chef Boyardee got canned.

If you get a chance, come see us perform live. It's like getting a hug from Venus de Milo.

We have a friend who is a psychiatrist for flies. He tries to help them get in touch with their inner maggots.

We don't mean to brag, but we invented that blue liquid they use to show absorbency in diaper commercials.

As the skunk philosopher once said, "I stink, therefore I am."

Here's a great joke to play next time you're on an airplane. Ask a flight attendant to introduce you to the captain. Then, when you meet the captain, frown and say, "But where's Tenille?"

They say laughter is the best medicine, so why not ask your HMO to reimburse you for the cost of this book?

About the Authors

Todd **Hafer** is director of product development and editorial services at Honor Books. He also tackles a variety of writing assignments for newspapers and magazines. He has won several national and international writing awards, a few of which his children haven't colored on or used to play army.

He enjoys competing in marathons and triathlons because "When you do something difficult and painful, it feels really good when you stop." His favorite activity, though, is spending time with his wife, Jody, and their four children, T.J., Jami, Taylor, and Olivia.

He also finds time for two other consuming passions: Lobbying to make tetherball an Olympic sport, and striving to create "a really good frozen waffle."

Jedd **Hafer** is a stand-up comic who has performed all over the country with people such as Tommy Chong, Pat Paulsen, Jimmy "J.J." Walker, Judi Tenuta, and Michael "Kramer" Richards. A finalist in the "Tonight Show With Jay Leno Comedy Challenge," Jedd is a two-time winner of the Colorado Young Writer's award, and his "Contests and Characters" sports humor column took top honors in a nationwide journalism contest.

Jedd's day job is site director at The Children's Ark, a home for troubled teens. He and his wife, Lindsey, are the parents of Brennan "The Boy" Hafer and Bryce "The Little Boy" Hafer.

Jedd would like to take this opportunity to address America's telemarketers: "My last name is pronounced with a long "A." Hay-fer. Rhymes with wafer. When there's a vowel, a consonant, then an E, the vowel assumes its long sound. You don't eat a vanilla waffer. You don't read a newspapper. Get it right, please. Thank you

A Note from the Editors

Guideposts, a nonprofit organization, touches millions of lives every day through products and services that inspire, encourage and uplift. Our magazines, books, prayer network and outreach programs help people connect their faith-filled values to their daily lives. To learn more, visit www .guideposts.com or www.guidepostsfoundation.org.